Music in North India

∞

EXPERIENCING MUSIC, EXPRESSING CULTURE

∞

GEORGE E. RUCKERT

New York   Oxford
Oxford University Press
2004

Oxford University Press

Oxford   New York
Auckland   Bangkok   Buenos Aires   Cape Town   Chennai
Dar es Salaam   Delhi   Hong Kong   Istanbul   Karachi   Kolkata
Kuala Lumpur   Madrid   Melbourne   Mexico City   Mumbai
Nairobi   São Paulo   Shanghai   Taipei   Tokyo   Toronto

Published by Oxford University Press, Inc.
198 Madison Avenue, New York, New York 10016
http://www.oup-usa.org

Library of Congress Cataloging-in-Publication Data
Ruckert, George.
    Music in North India : experiencing music, expressing culture / by George E.
Ruckert.
        p. cm.—(Global music series)
    Includes bibliographical references and index.
    ISBN 0-19-513993-3 (pbk.)
        1. Hindustani music—History and criticism. I. Title II. Series.

ML338.R83 2003
780'.954—dc21

                                                                              2003053588

Printing number: 9 8 7 6 5 4 3

Printed in the United States of America
on acid-free paper

GLOBAL MUSIC SERIES

General Editors: Bonnie C. Wade and Patricia Shehan Campbell

Music in East Africa, Gregory Barz
Music in Central Java, Benjamin Brinner
Teaching Music Globally, Patricia Shehan Campbell
Native American Music in Eastern North America, Beverley Diamond
Carnival Music in Trinidad, Shannon Dudley
Music in Bali, Lisa Gold
Music in Ireland, Dorothea E. Hast and Stanley Scott
Music in China, Frederick Lau
Music in Egypt, Scott Marcus
Music in Brazil, John Patrick Murphy
Music in America, Adelaide Reyes
Music in Bulgaria, Timothy Rice
Music in North India, George E. Ruckert
Mariachi Music in America, Daniel Sheehy
Music in West Africa, Ruth M. Stone
Music in the Andes, Thomas Turino
Music in South India, T. Viswanathan and Matthew Harp Allen
Music in Japan, Bonnie C. Wade
Thinking Musically, Bonnie C. Wade

Contents

Foreword

In the past three decades interest in music around the world has surged, as evidenced in the proliferation of courses at the college level, the burgeoning "world music" market in the recording business, and the extent to which musical performance is evoked as a lure in the international tourist industry. This heightened interest has encouraged an explosion in ethnomusicological research and publication, including the production of reference works and textbooks. The original model for the "world music" course—if this is Tuesday, this must be Japan—has grown old, as has the format of textbooks for it, either a series of articles in single multi-authored volumes that subscribe to the idea of "a survey" and have created a canon of cultures for study, or single-authored studies purporting to cover world musics or ethnomusicology. The time has come for a change.

This Global Music Series offers a new paradigm. Instructors can now design their own courses; choosing from a set of case study volumes, they can decide which and how much music they will teach. The series also does something else; rather than uniformly taking a large region and giving superficial examples from several different countries within it, case studies offer two formats—some focused on a specific culture, some on a discrete geographical area. In either case, each volume offers greater depth than the usual survey. Themes significant in each instance guide the choice of music that is discussed. The contemporary musical situation is the point of departure in all the volumes, with historical information and traditions covered as they elucidate the present. In addition, a set of unifying topics such as gender, globalization, and authenticity occur throughout the series. These are addressed in the framing volume, *Thinking Musically* (Wade), which sets the stage for the case studies by introducing those topics and other ways to think about how people make music meaningful and useful in their lives. *Thinking Musically* also presents the basic elements of music as they are practiced in musical systems around the world so that authors of each study do not have to spend time explaining them and can delve immediately into the particular music. A second framing volume, *Teaching Music Globally* (Campbell), guides teachers in the use of *Thinking Musically* and the case studies.

The series subtitle, "Experiencing Music, Expressing Culture," also puts in the forefront the people who make music or in some other way experience it and also through it express shared culture. This resonance with global studies in such disciplines as history and anthropology, with their focus on processes and themes that permit cross-study, occasions the title of this Global Music Series.

Bonnie C. Wade
Patricia Shehan Campbell
General Editors

Preface

Writing a big fat book on the music of North India would be a major project, but doable in its way. In such a book, one could at least bring the reader an acquaintance with the myriad of styles, genres, and practices that make up North India's huge patchwork quilt of musical traditions. In a short monograph such as this, it becomes much more difficult to make the big decisions: What can be left out? How can the theoretical descriptions be economized? Which musical examples will serve to give an introductory picture? How far can one go in describing the structures of *rāga* and *tāla*? Which artists will be representative? In which order can the musical idioms best be presented? And so on.

My experience as a sarod player, vocalist, and long-time teacher of both practical Hindustani classical music and world music classes has given me the impression that mixing musical exercises with a more traditional descriptive textbook approach would be the best way to introduce the music of North India. Most of these are rhythmic exercises, since learning melodic *rāga* involves more time than this short study can allow. In the hopes that the student will have time to practice these exercises during the course of study, they have been presented toward the beginning of the book, necessitating that the perhaps "more important" aspects of *rāga* and its realization come a bit later.

The music of India does not excerpt easily. It is very hard to convey a feeling for a *khyāl*, for instance, the same way one would introduce a Haydn minuet. The tonal language in the concept of *rāga* includes starting and stopping points, held-out notes, and a variety of melodic curves and twists, all of which defy short examples. For the best exposure, a listener cannot even rely on recordings, since these have their time restrictions as well—only a full concert can begin to convey the feeling for what a *rāga* performance is all about. But it is not always possible to get to a concert, and concerts of some of the more obscure genres may be nearly impossible for many readers to avail themselves of. So recordings are the next best thing, and the full CD recordings from which this book's excerpts are taken are all readily available to western listeners. It is hoped that instructors, librarians, and interested listeners will get a hold of the full recordings for a better perspective of the music described herein. They will provide a platform for a lifetime of exploration into a vast and wonderful musical ocean.

ACKNOWLEDGEMENTS

Many people have given much of their valuable time, services, and assistance to the preparation of this volume, and I could never have produced this volume without their help. Prime among the interviewees within has been Ali Akbar Khan, or "Khansahib," my own esteemed teacher, who, along with other teachers and friends, Swapan Chaudhuri and Zakir Hussain, gave extensive interviews, sharing their vast insights and feelings for the classical traditions.

The friends and colleagues at the Ali Akbar College have provided extensive assistance, notably Bruce Hamm and Sarah Morelli, who helped with digging up and reproducing photographs. Betsey Bruner, Tamarind Free Jones, and Susana Millman generously provided photographs as well.

The staff of the Music and Theater Arts Section at the Massachusetts Institute of Technology have been especially helpful with producing graphics, and I would like to especially thank Claries Snyder and Matt Agoglia for their help. Forrest Larsen has given us all a great gift with his CD mastering.

The many individuals who have generously provided their CDs for use in the musical illustrations are credited in the end of the book. I thank them all sincerely, along with the many artists whose work makes up so much of the experience to be found within.

Editor of the *Experiencing Music, Expressing Culture* series, Bonnie Wade, is my long-time friend and mentor, and without her patient guidance and advice with detailed proofreading, this volume would not have been realized.

And Gretchen, wondrous and beautiful wife and companion: could I ever begin to put it all in words?

CD Track List

1 Lata Mangeshkar sings *Mera Saya*. From *Great Artiste, Great Hits*, by Lata Mangeshkar. Used by permission of Saregama India Limited 1.32030.

2 *Jati chhand* exercise.

3 *Jati Laya* exercise.

4 Veda 1 *Rig Veda chant*. Used by permission of the publisher, Barenseiter-verlag.

5 Veda 2 *Sama Veda chant*. Used by permission of the publisher, Barenseiter-verlag.

6 Veda 3 *Yajur Veda chant*, showing vikriti patterns. Used by permission of the publisher, Barenseiter-verlag.

7 Dagar *Ālāp* in *Rag Todi*. Copyright 1999 by Raga Records.

8 Medium *jor* in *Rag Todi*. Copyright 1999 by Raga Records.

9 Fast *jor* in *Rag Todi*. Copyright 1999 by Raga Records.

10 & 11 Dara *dhrupad* and *bolbānt*s in *Rag Todi*. Copyright 1999 by Raga Records.

12 *Tarānā*.

13 *Meera Bhajan* by Anup Jalota. From *Bhajan Ganga*, Licensed by Universal Music India Pvt. Ltd., Mumbai India.

14 *Tongue Twister*. Used by permission of Ritesh Das, Toronto Tabla Ensemble.

15 *Gintī* 1 exercise.

16 *Gintī* 2 exercise.

17 *Gintī* 3 exercise.

18 *Tihāī* 1.

19 *Tihāī* 2.

20 *Tihāī* 3.

21 *Tihāī* 4.

22 *Tukrā.*

23 Alla Rakha, *chakradār* followed by *tipallī gat. Ustad Alla Rakha and Zakir Hussain Tabla Duet.* World Rights controlled by Precious Time Publishing (ASCAP), © Moment Records, Inc.

24 Rag *Gaur Sarang*: Asha Bhosle sings *chhotā khyāl.* CDF90691 Ali Akbar Khan and Asha Bhosle: Artists. Used by permission of AMMP Records.

25, 26, 27, 28, & 29 Rashid Khan, excerpts of khyal in *Bagesgri. Rashid Khan and Zakir Hussain.* World Rights controlled by Precious Time Publishing (ASCAP), © Moment Records, Inc.

30 Vilayat Khan, *gayaki* style *sitār* in *Sanj Sharavani. Vilayat Khan and Zakir Hussain.* World Rights controlled by Precious Time Publishing (ASCAP), © Moment Records, Inc.

31 Jankibai sings a ghazal in *Rag Bhairavi. Fana Kaisa Bana Kaisa,* from *Vintage Music from India.* Courtesy of Rounder Records (1-800-ROUNDER).

32, 33, 34, 35, & 36 Rag *Chandranandan*: Ali Akbar Khan plays sarod. CD 90002 Ali Akbar Khan: Artist/Composer. Used by permission of AMMP Records.

37 Nikhil Banerjee plays *sitār gat* in *Rag Sindhur Khammaj. 1972 Nikhil Banerjee Live in Amsterdam,* copyright 1993 by Raga Records.

38 Shivvkumar Sharma plays *santūr* in *Rag Rageshri. Pdt. Shivvkumar Sharma and Zakir Hussain.* World Rights controlled by Precious Time Publishing (ASCAP), © Moment Records, Inc.

39 Sultan Khan plays *sarangī* Rajasthani folk song. *Ustad Sultan Khan and Zakir Hussain.* World Rights controlled by Precious Time Publishing (ASCAP), © Moment Records, Inc.

40 Hariprasad Chaurasia plays *bānsurī* in *Rag Jāyashrī.* Track Courtesy of Navaras Records, UK, taken from NRCD 007 Hariprasad Chaurasia, Rag Jait.

41 *Sample This.* Used by permission of Ritesh Das, Toronto Tabla Ensemble.

42 *Marasim*: Jagit Singh sings modern *ghazal.* Used by permission of Sony Music India.

43 *Yellow Gal* by Krisha Bhatt and Jody Stecher. 1982. Used by permission of Jody Stecher.

CHAPTER 1

Modernity and Tradition

A CULTURE OF BEWILDERING VARIETY

I am leaning out of the rooming house window overlooking the intersection of Rashbehari Avenue and Gariahat Road in South Calcutta (new spelling, "Kolkata"). It is mid-morning, and I am a bit tired from a long overnight train ride, but sleep is out of the question—the noise of the traffic below me is deafening. Car, bus, and truck horns are blowing incessantly for no apparent reason at all, and if they give a moment's pause, the sound of a Lata Mangeshkar film song soars above the traffic from a small cassette player in the tobacconist's shop on the corner. The little speakers are tweaked at top volume, but Lata's clear and childlike voice is undaunted in its absolute determination to create an atmosphere of lilting and tearful film nostalgia in the tumult of Kolkata street life.

CD track 1, Lata Mangeshkar, Mera Saya
A short introduction uses synthesized chimes and strings in simple two-part harmony, playing in an eight-beat rhythm. This style of orchestration is common in film music of this era, and is somewhat reminiscent of the musical films of Hollywood in the 1930s. This award-winning song, composed by the renowned music director, Madan Mohan (d. 1975), uses parts of the classical rāga Anandi in its main melody, but departs from it in the musical interludes between verses.

    Lata begins by singing: Tu jahān jahan chalega mera sāya sātha hogā . . . *"Wherever you go, my shadow will be with you . . ."*

Taki mujhe ko yāda karake, jaba henge phiri ānsu, *"so, remembering me, whenever you have tears . . ."* Notice the *sweet ornament on the repeat of the word* mujhe. *Lata's precision with her voice is legendary, and greatly admired.*

Tabahi pe rokā lenge unhe ānke mere ānsu, *"I will stop them with my own." In this line, her delivery of* unhe ānke mere ānsu *is an emotional climax to the line, in which she pulls away her considerable vocal power and relaxes it with a melting softness which is one of her trademarks.*

Tu jidhar kā rukh karegā merā sāya, *"In whichever direction you go, there will be my shadow also . . ."*

I also awoke this morning to her voice on the train from Delhi—the famous Rajdhani Express—which tore through the unlit sleeping villages of the long Ganga plains all night long, with occasional stops at evocative and dimly lit stations such as Allahabad and Varanasi (Benares). It was Lata's voice which was the alarm clock on the train, heralding the serving of hot and welcome tea at the first sign of light. In India, one never gets too far from either tea or the sound of Lata's voice, although today it is mixed with other voices from the films, and popular selections from famous *ghazal* and *bhajan* singers, or the energetic *qawwalālīs* of the late Nusrat Fateh Ali Khan.

There was a time not so long ago when the songs from Indian films dominated the airwaves from Africa to Indonesia, and Lata was far and away the most frequently heard of the "playback singers." She is in the Guinness Book of Records for the most songs recorded (over six thousand). These singers sang the soundtracks for the majority of Indian films in the "Golden Age" (1950–1975), when every film had at least five songs, and the lead characters sang (or rather, lip-synched their singing with the playback singers' soundtrack) and danced, often in big production numbers *à la* MTV videos. The plots were simple: boy meets girl. They run into impossibly daunting social and political obstacles before heroically surmounting all barriers, convincing all that righteous and humble goodness is a joyous reason for rich and poor alike to sing and dance together. *Romeo and Juliet* with a happy ending. A small coterie of singers made virtually all of the music: Lata, Asha Bhosle, Mohammad Rafi, Mukesh, Talat Mahmood, Hemant Mukherjee, and a few others. The music had a life beyond the films, and even today, the

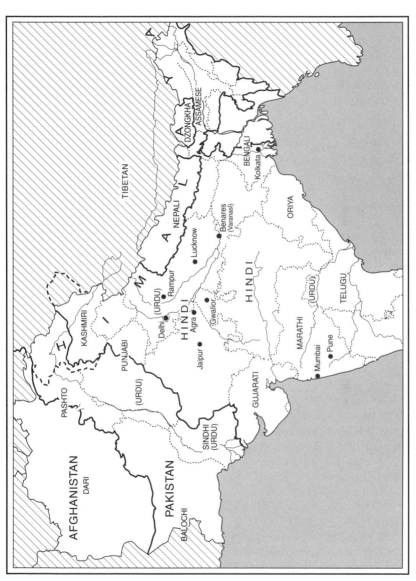

Map of Northern India with the major musical centers and historical courts that supported music shown by dots.

music enjoys a new life in hundreds of "greatest hits" CDs from these now-revered personalities.

The streets of Kolkata (Calcutta) are a parade of infinite variety and color. Kolkata is a huge city with people from all over India, indeed, all over the world. The English presence, from the long period of British residency in India (known as "The Raj"), is manifest to be romantically decaying in the state of the old and ornately impressive Victorian buildings. But these reminders of the past are being replaced by the steel, concrete, and glass of the present India, bursting to make known its brisk stride in the world economy. Old Bengali gentlemen, the "babus" of an earlier era, walk side by side with businessmen in western suits, and women in colorful saris and shalwars (dresses over cotton pajama pants) are accompanied by daughters in jeans. People love to be on the streets in India. It is a popular old social dance yet to be shut down by supermarkets, malls, and television.

Just down the street is a huge Krishna-Radha temple, drawing Hindu devotees and tourists alike to marvel at the gods and goddesses in the statuary of its teeming walls. Beneath the temple is an auditorium which hosts concerts of classical Indian music and dance by celebrated artists from all over India. Often the songs and dances will be about the same gods and myths depicted in the friezes of the temple. Around the corner is an Islamic mosque with a loudspeaker which today features a recording of a *muezzin*, singing to remind the faithful of the five-time daily ritual prayers. In the school across the street, the kids start the day singing a few patriotic songs, and even their version of the national anthem seems pretty rhythmically alive to me.

Anindya ("Anindo") is coming this morning at 10:30 to take me to the instrument-maker's shop. He is a young sarod (a type of lute) player, and a student of the great maestro Ali Akbar Khan. Anindya knows the music well, and he knows the musicians, and he knows the streets—all in all, the perfect companion for a trip through the mazes that India offers up in its fantastic geography, musical and otherwise.

Anindya arrives, and we have tea, which I have requested of the housekeeper. He starts right in with the Kolkata world of classical music. "Have you heard Amrita sing?" he asks, and I shake my head no. "She is the student of Pandit-ji (a Hindu term of respect for a senior teacher of music), and everyone is talking about her. She is singing at my cousin's house in Lake Market tonight, and you must come." Such informal house concerts are quite common. And he continues on about Kolkata's main music festival. "No, Khansahib ("-sahib" is a Muslim suffix of respect) is not playing at Dover Lane this year. But Ajoy-bhai is singing the first night, and Hari-ji closes the festival, and Zakir-bhai is playing with him." He uses these familiar and respectful endings "-ji" (affectionate respect) and "-bhai" (literally, "brother") to refer to the artists by first name. (These suffixes are often used within Indian families, and the music world is thought of as a big family.) If it is happening in the classical music scene here, Anindya will know, and this is important to me, because that is why I have come here to North India's musical capital city.

There are other cities in which one can pursue classical music, but in a land where this music was heard only in courts and temples for hundreds of years, the urban centers of Mumbai (Bombay), Pune, Delhi, Varanasi, and Kolkata are the specific cities where most of the artists have chosen to live. Elsewhere in North India, classical music is less available. Film and popular music dominate the musical fare, yet there is ever the strong presence of devotional songs. And each region offers its own traditions—ranging from theater songs of Maharashtra, songs of the Bengal poet Rabindranath Tagore, or the numerous genres of "folk" songs, any of which may offer the subtle and expressive refinements of vital traditions that often date back to antiquity. India is big (a billion people in this twenty-first century). India is old (evidence of musical activity dates back four thousand years). And India is filled with contradictions.

"Go ahead, say something wrong about India."

I am having lunch in the cafeteria of MIT with a graduate student, recently arrived from India. He has a charm and a twinkle in his eye, as if he's played this game of daring-the-questioner many times before.

"I mean, ignoring geographical position, say something wrong about India, and I will contradict you and show you how the opposite of whatever you say is true."

I can only think of small things to offer—like suggesting India as responsible for the origin of wearing a tie or dancing a polka—suddenly unsure if the vast profusion of scarves or dances in India could be construed as "tie" or "polka." Furthermore, I see his point: India is big enough to embrace many climates and geographies; old enough to have seen thousands of changes in science, culture, and politics; and diverse enough to have contradictions at every level of social behav-

ior: from poverty to wealth, unsophisticated simplicity to es-
oteric sophistication, simple rustic rituals to complex philo-
sophical spirituality
    I respond "You could just as easily ask me to say some-
thing correct about India, and then go about proving me
wrong."
    He laughs. "Exactly my point. And the source of many
of India's problems, er, contemporary challenges (he smiles
with this understanding of modern political correctness of
speech). You see what today's scientists, businessmen, and
politicians have to deal with. Even in your world of music,
there is no one common ground in India. It is simply too vast
a topic to bring under one umbrella. And for the last several
hundred years, India has been absorbing the West as well.
We now have all the modern trappings, from computers to
air pollution. You can just listen to the music coming out of
India and you can easily see hear we're talking about."

In speaking of the music of India, one uses several large categories. The north-south division of India's languages implies the main one: in the vast linguistic area of the north, those languages derived from Sanskrit—Hindi-Urdu, Maharati, Gujarati, Punjabi, Bengali, and others; in the large southern geographical region, the Dravidian-derived languages—Tamil, Telegu, Malayalam, and Kannada. Analogous to this linguistic division lie the main differences in style between what are called the Hindustani (northern) and Karnatak (southern) musical styles, which began to be distinguishable from roughly the thirteenth century. In fact, between these broad divisions, much overlapping and exchange of musical materials has taken place. The long history of regional musical styles makes it difficult to simply divide India into North and South.

    Another way of looking at stylistic diversity in India's music is through the so-called "Great Tradition" and the "Little Traditions." The former includes what we in the West think of as theorized, or "classical," styles that overspan many smaller regions. "Little Traditions," or regional styles, are often very old and supremely refined, but are associated with specific areas (Rajasthani folk song, for example), and often cities and towns (e.g., the *raslila* theater of Varanasi). This text, however, provides insufficient space to discuss these regional styles.

THREADS TO FOLLOW IN THIS TEXT

The immense weave of music emerging from North India does in fact show it all, as the discussion with the graduate student suggests, and seeking to narrow the focus in order to describe a few styles and genres will naturally do injustices to the many which are left out. It is better to speak of a few features that wind their way through the music of many styles and discuss how they interrelate. I have chosen three aspects of the music to follow throughout this book: devotion, the compositional/improvisational balance, and the use of the syllable.

The Devotional Component. One aspect which is clearly identifiable in Indian music is the devotional component. India's mystic philosophies are at once universal (and eagerly pursued throughout the world) and sectarian. The strife between various religious sects in India runs the gamut from highly volatile and militantly confrontational, to daily and tolerant interrelating with an often and sublime mutual understanding. But, all groups share the fervent and endless expression of religious feeling in their musical outpouring.

Fixed Composition and Improvisation. Another thread which we can use to help hear what is behind musical expression in India is the balance between fixed composition and improvisation—preservation and creation. What better reveals this than the concept and performance of that elusive and charming musical format called "*rāga*"? (Throughout the book, I will be using the ancient Sanskrit-language form of the word "*rāga*" alongside its more modern Hindi-language form, "*rāg*.") The young West has eagerly pursued various derivatives of *rāga*, including "rāga-rock," "rāga-jazz," and "New Age rāga"; these have merely skimmed the surface of what is a fascinating interplay of prescribed melodic movement and on-the-spot composition. Texture plays an important role, with implications that are at once social, musical, and pedagogic; the texture in nearly all of the music is either monophonic or heterophonic, and accommodates the ideas and working out of ornamental melodies and variations that are so much a part of the Indian musical mind. (For discussion of the basic elements of music and terminology, see Wade, *Thinking Musically*, in this Global Music Series.)

The question, "What is a rāga?", taken up in Chapter 5, is often the first one that arises in the discussion of the music of India. In many cases, the essence of a particular rāg

can be effectively reduced to its scale-form. In most others such a reduction is neither possible or desirable, since a medley of melodic units within the scale are basic to its realization. "After you learn many songs and compositions in a rāga, you will begin to see how it is constructed," says Ali Akbar Khan. "From just stating the theoretical structures, you will only get a partial view. Each rāga takes a lifetime to learn . . . sometimes more than one lifetime."

The Verbal Syllable. A third thread focuses on the verbal syllable. We can watch this at work from the naming of the pitches, to the abstract patterns of drum and dance, to the disintegration of a song text in performance. The meaning of music is often abstracted beyond the syntactical meaning of words, and most musicians spend their artistic life in finding this point of balance between a syllable's verbal evocation and its utility in rhythmic combination and textural abstraction. One can hardly think of the world of drumming, dance, and instrumental music without seeing the working out of these syllabic ideas. Here I shall introduce you to two significant examples of verbal syllables. Others occur in later chapters.

Rhythmic Jātīs. Syllables are used by many musicians as rhythmic *jātīs* (types) to construct rhythmic patterns. (The *jātī* system is used to structure rhythmic theory in Karnatak music and has entered North Indian practice by the way of dancers and their accompanying musicians.) Each syllable is used to stand for one beat (or a microbeat, depending on the context), and these are grouped in patterns from one to nine units long (Figure 1.1). The words appear to

Number of beats	Syllables	Grouping
1	ta	
2	taka	
3	takita	
4	takadimi	
5	taka takita	2 + 3
6	taka takadimi	2 + 4
7	takita takadimi	3 + 4
8	takita takita taka	3 + 3 + 2
9	taka takita takadimi	2 + 3 + 4

FIGURE 1.1   *The rhythmic* jātīs *articulated with syllables.*

become long and tongue twisting, but the component syllables for the last five *jātīs* are simply groupings of the first four. Figure 1.1 lays out the *jātī* system, and then Activities 1.1 and 1.2 provide you with a chance to understand how they apply to musical situations.

ACTIVITY 1.1 *Reciting the* jātīs *as rhythmic groupings (CD track 2)*
Say each jātī *four times in rapid succession, going from one to nine and back to one, nonstop, with no pauses between the* jātīs. *Clap on the first syllable of each. In the diagram below, an x represents a clap, and the voice continues its recitation as fast as is possible. Going up from one to nine, the claps become farther apart, and coming down they become closer together:*

Claps: x   x   x   x   x   x   x   x   x
Voice: ta ta ta ta ta ka ta ka ta ka ta ka ta ki
Claps: x   x   x   x
Voice: ta ta ki ta ta ki ta ta ki ta ta ka di mi . . .

ACTIVITY 1.2 *Reciting the* jātīs *as changes in speed (CD track 3)*
This time keep the claps slow and evenly spaced and recite each jātī *four times as in Activity 1.1. Beyond the first* jātī *the rhythmic space between the claps will be subdivided by the numbers. Again, go from one to nine and back:*

Claps: x   x   x   x   x   x
Voice: ta   ta   ta   ta   ta   ka   ta   ka . . .

The first exercise (Activity 1.1) illustrates the grouping of a regular pulse, called the *chhand* by many musicians. The pulse, in this case one syllable per beat, is grouped into four groups of one, four groups of two, four groups of three, and so on, in succession. The second exercise (Activity 1.2) illustrates the idea of relative speed, known as the *laya*. In classical Indian music, the fabric of the rhythm is made up of the interplay between *chhand* and *laya*. It would be relatively common for any classical instrumentalist to interpret these syllables as strokes on his or her instrument. An accomplished dancer would be expected to fashion a composition on the spot from say, *khanda jātī* (five), and a trained drummer (most likely a *tablā* player in North India) would be able to follow along without verbal explanation of the rhythm. Players of the *sitār* and *sarod* (the most common of the classical stringed instruments) routinely use these rhythms to structure their improvisations in rāga.

Syllables for Pitch Names. Another use of the syllable is quite familiar to most musicians: the use of syllables for pitch names. In the European tradition, we say do, re, mi, fa, sol, la, ti, do. In India, musicians say **sa, re, ga, ma, pa, dha, ni, sa**. As in the "movable do" system, **sa** is relative (rather than designating a specific pitch), and can begin anywhere. Each person has a range where **sa, re, ga** . . . is comfortable to sing. A sitārist might tune to western pitch D, a sarodist to C, and a flutist may have a collection of instruments of different sizes, each tuned to a different *sa*. In the interest of simplicity, one can place **sa** at C, and thus the major scale (C, D, E, F, G . . .) can be sung "**sa, re, ga,** . . . and so forth." (If you are singing in a group it might be easier for everybody to sing the higher notes if you choose the pitch A as **sa**. The note C will be used as *sa* to avoid writing sharps and flats for the major scale.) Once **sa** is established for a particular voice or instrument, **sa** and **pa**, the first and fifth degrees, are fixed and never altered; all the other notes have two forms, so that there are twelve in all, much like the Western chromatic scale. Figure 1.2 is a notation chart with the note names and equivalent pitch placements. In the use of roman letters, the lower case letter stands for the lower form of a note.

S	sa	sadja	स	C
r	re	komal rishab	रि	D♭
R	re	shuddh rishab	रि	D
g	ga	komal gandhar	ग	E♭
G	ga	shuddh gandhar	ग	E
m	ma	shuddh madhyam	म	F
M	ma	tivra madhyam	मं	F♯
P	pa	pancham	प	G
d	dha	komal dhaivat	ध	A♭
D	dha	shuddh dhaivat	ध	A
n	ni	komal nishad	नि	B♭
N	ni	shuddh nishad	नि	B

FIGURE 1.2 *Key to notation*

Any melody can be sung with the melodic syllables, which is called "singing in *sārgām*." For example, Figure 1.3 is what the first line of "My Country 'Tis of Thee" looks like when written in *sārgām*.

S S R | N ˍS R | G G m | G ˍR S | R S N | S — —
My country 'tis of thee, etc.

FIGURE 1.3   *"My Country 'tis of Thee" in* sārgām *notation.*

The dot below the note means it is in the lower register; upper register notes indicate a dot above. The letters stand for the pitches, the vertical bars indicate divisions of the *tāl* (meter), and the loops indicate that the beat is subdivided into twos, threes, or fours. A dash looks like a rest, but usually indicates that the previous note is sustained through it.

THE OLD AND THE NEW IN AN ANCIENT LAND

We return to Kolkata. Anindya leads me through the crowded streets to a little shop—a stall, really—that is like a small store with no front wall facing the busy street. Inside are three workers sitting on the floor, and numerous instruments—*sarods, sitārs,* and *tanpuras*—hang from hooks above them. These are all covered with the dust of the streets, so they look like they could have been there for twenty years, although some are brand new. Anindya gestures for me to sit on a bench in the front of the shop. Hemen Sen, who owns the shop, is an older man who sits near the open door surrounded by his tools (see Figure 1.4). He places himself here to greet customers, but he is a master luthier, and only reluctantly turns from the work on an instrument to make conversation. Hemen-ji is one of the most renowned instrument makers in India, and I am awed by the fact that I am sitting on the bench where so many of India's finest instrumentalists have sat to place their orders with this great and humble craftsman. His English is minimal, and I am still learning Bengali, so we will converse through Anindya. I am there to order a *sarod.* When Hemen-ji asks about my background, Anindya assures him that I will require a first-class instrument—this kind of personal touch is still quite important—and it is communicated to me that I must return next year at this time, and my instrument will be ready for me. Done.

Hemen-ji does not want or need to hear from me the qualities the instrument must have, for he is the authority and will bring an instrument to life with his own hands. Of course he would listen if I said that

FIGURE 1.4 *Hemen Sen, master luthier, sits on the floor of his small shop in south Kolkata. Instrumentalists from all over India, and indeed, the world, come to Hemen-ji for* sitārs, sarods, *and* tanpuras.

my hands were big or small, or that I had a special need. For my part, I am just grateful that he is willing to take my order, because he has a waiting list and could easily give me an instrument made by an assistant. The range in musical quality which an instrument might possess is shared the world over, but in India it is exacerbated by the fact that there really is no standard. *Sitārs* come in all sizes, as do *sarods, tablās,* and *tānpuras.* The quality of the woods and other materials used and the level of craftsmanship vary enormously, ranging from the brilliant sonorous instruments of a maker like Hemen, to the *sitār*-shaped street souvenirs of the tourist traps. To get a good instrument, in a word, is a crapshoot.

FIGURE 1.5 *Hemen Sen's instrument shop. One of Hemen-ji's assistants inspects a newly-finished* sitār. *Two* sitārs *and two instrumental* tānpurās *hang on the right, and a corner of a new* sarod *is visible in the lower left. Pictures of famous players of Hemen's instruments line the walls.*

In Hemen's shop (Figure 1.5), everything is done with hand tools, as it probably has been since *sitārs* and *sarods* were first made. And yet, so much that was inconceivable a short while ago is now changing in the world of Indian music. A vast culture that was steeped in traditional ways, where music and musicians had definite social positions in the hierarchy, has now become electrified with the power and ready availability of the socially homogenizing media of the twenty-first century. This has had sweeping effects in the music world, where it is not so much that boundaries have been crossed but rather that they have been completely erased in a few generations. In a culture that had long fostered and supported a hierarchical social system, generation after generation of Indian aristocracy nurtured the classical music as their own in a refined palace life of the privileged few. The millions of people beyond that context were not exposed to the classical traditions. Somewhat abruptly in 1947, although most people had seen the writing on the wall, these royal courts that had persisted even in the British colonial period were dissolved by the newly declared independent democracy that is modern India. The classical musicians were forced to more earnestly cultivate the patronage of an urban middle class. In this market place, they found that their art was challenged by the enchanting stars of the flourishing behemoth film industry, as well as diverse musical influences from all over the world.

The social change from a feudal agricultural society to that of a modern urban democracy has proceeded for decades in various stages throughout India, but millions of people still live a lifestyle that retains elements of very old tradition. For the musicians, the change has been quite dramatic. Being a court musician meant an elite life of dedication to music alone, with that expanded sense of time that India has cultivated both philosophically and artistically. Today, when a musician walks into the musical scene, he is expected to bear with him recordings and a concert appeal, both in appearance and popular presentation that will make him or her endearing. Whereas in the past, a community or audience would know a performer's style, and would look for some new approach to an established repertory, now he or she will take a position on a different stage for two hours night after night, and the audience will expect to be treated to a "full show."

How different was the reception when classical musicians first "came out" to the public in the early twentieth century? The great singer Vishnu Digambar Paluskar was one of the first to present a public concert in the early 1900s. People on the side of the old aristocratic culture hissed and threw stones as he left the hall because they regarded classical music as the province of the privileged classes and questioned his right to take his music to the public. It was "their" music, and had been fostered by and for them for as long as anyone remembered. "Pearls before swine," was the attitude, and they scorned the public concert as just another corruption of the intruding British way of life. The whole idea of *buying* a concert ticket was a prostitution of the sacred art. When Rukmini Devi presented her classical dance (*Bharata Natyam*) on stage in 1935, she too was censured. She was an upper-class Brahmin performing a dance of a lower-class—and of a caste (*devadāsī*) of suspect moral character in the British view at that—and she was dancing on a public stage of all places (not even in a drawing room before a select audience). (For a discussion of the *devadāsī* tradition see Viswanathan and Allen's *Music of South India* in this Global Music Series.) The famous vocalist Kesarbai Kerkar, who died in the 1960s, refused to sing in a concert where the public paid for tickets. If she did perform in public, it was only at a *sponsored* concert—a concert where a patron paid the artists, and the tickets were distributed to those who requested them, or provided on a "membership" basis.

The patronized concert became very popular as the courts were in decline in the first half of the twentieth century. A patron, or a group of people dedicated to the arts, would get together and provide or raise money for a music festival, inviting artists from all over North India to sing in a chain of recitals all day and all night for three or four days. Continuing past independence in 1947, many of the festivals took place in the most populous cities, ensuring that the music would be accessible to a vast number of people. A star-system emerged, where the most popular and entertaining personalities became leading lights, driving artists' fees upward. Today economic difficulties, coupled with the public's changing preferences for shorter programs, have closed most of these festivals, although most major cities still host at least one classical music festival each year. These are a series of concerts over four or five days, often featuring at least one all-night performance, in which, ironically, the more popular musicians appear in the wee hours of the morning.

In former eras at the courts, musicians would live among the people before whom they played and sang. Their practice and presentations were more open to regular scrutiny. Of course the more tedious aspects of practice—the hours of repetitious exercises and the learning of new pieces—took place behind closed doors, but the musical performance itself was designed and presented like an open practice. The resulting musical display is known today by the name of the musical format, *rāga*, which is further discussed in a later chapter.

In the modern concert hall numerous changes continue to affect the style of performance: musicians are dependent upon electronic sound reinforcement, and audiences expect that concerts will begin and end at certain preassigned times. They wish to be entertained, but not overburdened with recondite technical or musical displays. They want to hear a polished and virtuosic performance, but not too introspective an exploration—they cannot perceive the minute differences between the hundreds of *rāga* and *tāla* types to which former elite audiences may have been more attuned.

Some of the changes have been brought about by the recording industry. In the early years, an artist would have only a few minutes to sing, and hence the longer classical styles were not thought of as appropriate for recording. A song that lasted from two to five minutes could be polished for recorded presentation. Much more difficult is the unfolding of a *rāga*, where the timing of unfolding and exploration play such an important role. While a *rāga* performance might include materials requiring lengthy improvised development that can be edited out of a recording, the end product is nevertheless expected to have the same polish as the fixed material of the more normal fare of popular music. This affects a performer's presentation and repertory, for on a recording or even in concert he or she will wish to present only what sounds best . . . the polishing of a "sonic object," as one might prepare a Mozart sonata for recording.

INDIAN MUSIC ON THE MOVE

The spreading of Indian music all over the globe has had a great effect on many genres of the music. For the classical artists, it has meant the development of new audiences who have greeted the music with respect and enthusiasm sometimes lacking for them at home. Instrumental music, where the language problems of song texts are not encountered, has flourished. Western audiences have participated in the elevation of the *tablā* player, who in India was traditionally regarded as a second-class accompanist.

The great movement of Indian people to the West (especially Europe, Canada, and the United States) has spread appreciation of the popular genres as well. Second generations of these emigrants have added driving percussion tracks, bass lines, and even hip-hop special effects to popular and film music already vital in its rhythmic component. These doctored recordings are termed "remixes" and can be readily available at some specialty stores. But since most of these use previously recorded materials without licensing or permission, they are illegal, and cannot be sold through normal commercial channels. Nor could an example be included in this collection for the same reason.

Internationalization has been of prime importance in many musicians' training in all styles: Indian classical musicians have taught their music in centers all over the world, and many have settled outside of India. Now a number of artists of non-Indian origin are taking their place in the concert schedules; conductors such as Seiji Ozawa and Zubin Mehta conduct major western orchestras, while Kiri Te Kanawa, Midori, and Yo Yo Ma are musical artists of the European tradition. National origin is no longer a criterion for identifying musical style: "Indian" musicians now have non-Indian names (Ken Zuckerman, Steve Gorn, and others) and a wide following. And to many music lovers around the world, Ravi Shankar, Ali Akbar Khan, Zakir Hussain, and others are regular musical fare.

The question may come to your mind: why is this music attractive beyond its national boundaries? What are the qualities that are unique to this music, and what is shared by the music of other cultures? With the idea of keeping the devotional component, the fixed-improvised attitude, and the verbal syllable as fundamentals, I will start with the idea of "affect," or the feelings and moods, as well as the ideas associated with its "inner meanings" in the next chapter. Chapter 3 discusses some of the social factors in the music. Chapter 4 examines the rhythmic structures, and Chapter 5 the melodic formats. In Chapter 6 there is a discussion of the great variety of instrumental timbres, and a look past the traditional styles to some of the popular and mixed modes is discussed in Chapter 7.

CHAPTER 2

Affect

The term "affect" refers to the feeling for music held by both musician and audience. In India, it embraces the musical moods, the feelings of time theory (in which the *rāgas* are associated with a time of day or season), song texts, religious connotations, and the musicians' attitudes towards their training, along with a notion of the sentiments found in devoted practice.

RELIGIOUS CONNOTATIONS

The question of what is religious and what is secular presents us with the classic razor's edge of discrimination in many cultures and their musics. Among musicians in India it is a well-worn topic—and a continuing discussion that reveals many points of view. India is a country that is dominated by Hindu traditions, but there are several millions of Muslims as well as Christians, Parsis, Jains, Sikhs, and Jews—as well as a vast number of people who claim no particular religion. The musicians are themselves representatives of every point of view. In the medieval courts, especially during the Mughal dynasty (1526–1857), there were many musicians who converted to Islam in order to secure a court position; many of the musicians who have "Khan" as a last name were associated with a Moslem court and may well have converted from Hinduism.

No matter what the practicing faith of a musician might be, most acknowledge the music's origin as a divine manifestation, a gift from God, which is a profound root of its affect. The Hindus will call this aspect of the music *Nād-Brahmā*, "sound as God," or "the language of God." The purpose of serious music, then, is to bring oneself in tune with the highest planes, and the practice of music is like a prayer. The musician is on a lifelong path (*mārga*) which has spiritual overtones, mixed with the *yoga* ("yoke") of refinement, knowledge, and purification. Hindus would add that this leads to *mukti*, or "liberation," "release." Although these ideas are part of the Hindu tradition, one does not hear them contradicted by musicians of other faiths. On the contrary, these principles are often found in the song texts, especially in the texts of songs designed to teach young musicians about the nature of the musical experience. The following anonymous song text tells of the famous sixteenth-century singer, Tansen (d. 1586), of the court of Akbar the Great (r. 1556–1605).

Nāda samudra ko . . .
Mankind cannot reach across the infinite ocean of musical Sound.
The instruction of the wise is to learn the rhythmic compositions
*   of both the saints and the music of the folk.*
Various schools have interpreted the mysteries of music,
*   meditating on the works of Brahmā, Vishnu, and Shivā.*
Praising the teachers who unraveled these secrets,
Tansen's song melted the stones with melody.

SACRED TEXTS

The oldest scriptures in India are known as the *Vedas*, a word that literally means "knowledge." Dating perhaps from 1500 BCE, they are four in number (*Rig, Sāma, Yājur,* and *Atharva Vedas*), and are comprised of sacred hymns, poetic descriptions of the gods and nature, rituals, and blessings. Originally, they were passed on orally, memorized by an initiated class of priests (*Brahmins*), and the very act of hearing them was considered auspicious; understanding their profound philosophical implications was not immediately foremost. This feeling of the sacredness in simply hearing has become basic to the Indian musical ideal.

To be sure, the meaning of these Vedic texts is important, and extensive commentaries, such as the *Upanishads, Brahmānas, Aranyakas,* and *Purānas* explicate in great detail the philosophical and theological facets of the Vedic message (collectively called *Vedantā*). But for musicians, it was the sound of the language, Sanskrit, which was preeminent, with specific emphasis on the independent syllables of that language. Especially important among these was the syllable *om,* sometimes spelled *āum,* which stands for the sound of the infinite and eternal cosmos itself.

OM
The essence of beings is the earth;
the essence of the earth is water;
the essence of water is plants;
the essence of plants is man;
the essence of man is speech;
the essence of speech is Rig *verse;*
the essence of Rig *verse is* Sāman *chant;*
the essence of Sāman *chant is the quintessence of all essences;*
it is the highest, the ultimate
OM.

Chāndogya Upanishad

CD track 4 is an example of Vedic chant, a hymn to the god Kubera, guardian of the gods' treasury (from the *Rig Veda*). Note that the chanting is syllabic (one syllable for each pitch). The Brahmin priest recites the text basically on one note, ornamenting with a note above and a note below. This creates a droning sound that could have been a seed for the larger concept of the drone characteristic in classical music. The rhythm of the text is important—the alternations of long and short syllables that become the later basis for the *tāl* system (see Chapter 4).

A very different style of rendering the text can be heard in CD track 5 from the *Sāma-Veda*. The text is not particularly emotional, but the chanter uses a greater range in pitch, elongates and repeats the syllables, and produces an emotional rendering of a sacred text that might not immediately suggest such outpouring. Here the priest repeats the opening words and extends the syllables over several pitches (*melisma*). We begin to hear the ancient roots to modern musical style—the *Sama Veda* is considered to be one of the historical origins of musical language. Some of the features, which later characterize the classical traditions, can be seen in nascent form in this style of chant:

- It was chanted from memory only by specialists (an oral tradition).
- A single, unaccompanied melodic line used all seven notes.
- Simply hearing these chants was considered auspicious (*Nād-Brahmā*).
- The syllable became a central focus of the sound (over the textual meaning).
- Tropes (verbal insertions), repetitions, and *vikriti* (see following) patterns were used.

VERBAL SYLLABLES

The focus on the syllable gets special treatment in the process of re-ordering, known as *vikriti* ("crooked"). *Vikriti* patterns reorder the sylla-bles of the chant in a way that the meaning becomes completely lost in a mathematical permutation process. Each reordering pattern has a name, and the ones heard on CD track 6, treating a text from the *Yajur Veda*, are

1. *Krama*, in which the syllables are reordered thus: 1-2, 2-1, 2-3, 3-2 . . . and so on.
2. *Jatā*, which is 1-2 2-1 1-2, 2-3 3-2 2-3 . . . and so on.
3. *Ghana*, which is 1-2 2-1 1-2-3 3-2-1 1-2-3, 2-3 3-2 2-3-4 4-3-2 2-3-4 . . . and so on.

While it may be difficult to follow the precise ordering of the text, the repetition of syllables can be easily heard as the Brahmin systematically puts them through reordered sequences. This attention to development of long and short syllables would later be given extensive treatment in the classical traditions.

ACTIVITY 2.1 Vikriti *patterns*
Practice these simple phrases and reorder the syllables according to the krama, jatā, *and* ghana *patterns: a) "Simple Simon met a pieman . . ." or b) "Do unto others as you . . ."*

1. *Krama:*
   a) sim-ple ple-sim, ple-si si-ple, si-mon mon-si, mon-met met-mon . . .
   b) do-un un-do, un-to to-un, to-oth oth-to, oth-ers ers-oth . . .
2. *Jatā:*
   a) sim-ple ple-sim sim-ple, ple-si, si-ple ple-si . . .
   b) do-un un-do do-un, un-to to-un un-to, to-oth oth-to to-oth . . .
3. *Ghana:*
   a) sim-ple ple-sim sim-ple-si si-ple-sim sim-ple-si, ple-si si-ple ple-si-mon mon-sim-ple ple-si-mon . . .
   b) do-un un-do do-un-to to-un-do do-un-to, un-to to-un un-to-oth oth-to-un un-to-oth . . .

Now invent your own phrase and practice it with vikriti *patterns.*

From the exercise in Activity 2.1, even though the sentence becomes totally nonsensical, one can get an impression of one type of compositional process which is very ancient in its origin: that of the systematic permutation of syllables to create new patterns while retaining the old ones. It is an exercise requiring both sharp memory and intense concentration. Imagine that the syllables were the names of the notes, plucking patterns on stringed instruments, drum sounds, or dance steps, and you have grasped one of the very important traditional ways of creating a composition. Normally the syllables used in these latter media are much fewer in number than those of everyday speech or scripture, and they are often chosen for their ease in creating rapid patterns (see the *jātī* exercises, Activities 1.1 and 1.2, for example).

The syllable can be used in other ways to create a composition with words, but without "meaning" in the conventional sense of that word. Remember that sound itself implies a divine presence. Sanskrit syllables also carry sacred etymological implications. So while some singing has no translatable meaning in the sense of logical sentences, there is often a higher sense of meaning in the sound of the song itself. Hence, communication of the affect of vocal music is not always dependent on meaningful song texts.

The Vocal Genre of dhrupad. In the style of singing known as *dhrupad* (the oldest currently performed classical style), the artist begins by intoning the abstract vocables *"ta na e na ri re ra na nom tom"* in a somewhat random order. Later the vocables will be sung fast, in a manner reminiscent of scat singing in jazz. Legends trace these to old sacred *mantrās*, prayer-like formulas which might have originally been *ananta hari om* ("bliss-God-om"), or *om tu narayana hari* ("om, thou Lord, Vishnu"). Whatever their original meaning, it is lost in the random reordering of the sounds.

The use of syllables helps singers with phrasing and vocal timbre. In CD tracks 7-8-9, the famous late dhrupad artists, Aminuddin and Moinuddin Dagar, sing part of the *ālāp* or introduction, to *rāg Todi*. The *ālāp* (literally, "conversation") presents the rāga, first note-by-note, then phrase-by-phrase, very slowly and patiently expanding the range to include the higher register. It begins without a regular rhythmic pulse, and then a second part progresses from a slow rhythm (*jor*, "momentum") to a faster one at the conclusion of the movement. The artists use the syllables in a random reordering of *ta na e na ri re ran na nom tom*. This style of singing is simply called *"nom-tom."* The *ālāp* movement may continue for an hour or more, as the artists seek to soak the atmosphere with the mood of the *rāg*, presenting all its features gradually. Figure 2.1 will

Part 1. CD track 7. In this first excerpt of the ālāp, *the flatted second degree of the scale,* komal *re, is presented. The singers use the notes below the* re, *but not those above. Notice the use of the* nom–tom *syllables and the careful intonation. The whole performance, from which this is an excerpt, introduces each note in ascending order up the scale.*

Part 2. CD track 8. This is the jor *section. The music has a rhythmic pulse, but no regular meter (and no drum accompaniment). The artists use the syllables to create phrasing and bring rhythmic life to the more-or-less abstract phrases.*

Part 3. CD track 9. This is the fast jor *that concludes the* ālāp. *Now the syllables are rapidly repeated, almost simulating an instrumental style. After the 0:09 mark, Moinuddin Dagar begins a powerful shaking ornamental style called* gamak. *At the 0:18 mark he explains (for this is an informal house concert) that this vocal technique is different from how it might sound in* khyāl *style, in which the same melodic run would be sung on a vowel without* nom–tom *inflection (i.e., "n-n-n-n-n-n-na").*

A dhrupad *(CD track 10) is literally a composition in* tāla *based on a fixed text (hence the name, "dhrupad," from* dhruva, *"fixed," and* pada, *"verse"). These old* dhrupad *compositions are sung the same way each time and highly venerated, for in their fixity (unlike improvised music), they maintain traditional ideas of* rāg *configuration. This song has an introspective devotional text:* kauna barama bhule . . . *("Who are you to think of yourself as knowledgeable and wise . . ."). It is accompanied by the elongated, barrel-shaped double-headed drum, the* pakhāwaj, *and is in a medium-slow twelve-beat cycle (in which the downbeat playfully falls on the normally unaccented second syllable of the word* barama).*

The fixed composition lasts until the 1:24 mark. At this point the excerpt changes to the final section, CD track 11, the bolbānt *("word division"), in which the text is parsed into rhythmic syllables and the artists improvise patterns in the* tāl. *All meaning of the text is secondary to the rhythmic use of verbal syllable.*

FIGURE 2.1 *Listening guide:* dhrupad *performance.*

guide you through CD tracks 7-11, beginning with the *ālāp* but proceeding beyond it to let you hear the structural elements of a performance of *dhrupad*.

The *dhrupad* style manifests a performance pattern followed in most North Indian classical music: a slow abstract beginning gathers momentum, "restarts" with a fixed composition, and climaxes with a fast rhythmic section.

The Vocal Genre of Tarānā. The rhythmic syllable/vocable is a prominent part of another genre of vocal composition as well: the *tarānā*, CD track 12. The sources for the tarānā syllables are the *nom-tom ālāp*, mixed with some of the syllables from dance, instrumental music, drumming, and some others which are unique to the genre itself. A *tarānā* is often sung as a concluding item of a *rāga* performance, since most are rendered at a fast tempo and can be quite exciting. CD track 12 is an excerpt from a very old and traditional *tarānā* in the late-night *rāg Adāna*. You can first hear the *tablā* (played by Swapan Chaudhuri), then the *tānpurā* (drone) in the background, and a shadowing instrument, the bowed *sarangī*, played by Ramesh Misra. The famous light-classical singer Asha Bhosle sings the first part, the "home" section, called the *asthāī*. At the 0:55 mark, a second, higher section begins called the *antarā*. Division into these two sections is a common way of structuring fixed compositions, and to a lesser extent, improvisations, as well.

SONG TEXTS

On the other side of the spectrum of the abstract vocables lie the song texts that convey meaning. Meaningful Hindi (or Urdu—they are essentially the same language written in different scripts, although the Persian ancestors of Urdu have contributed a large vocabulary to modern Hindi-Urdu) song texts fall into three broad categories. The first includes genres with devotional texts, such as *dhrupads, bhajans,* and *qawwālīs*. The second category are those which have love as their primary topic, although the dividing line between human love and divine love is often blurred—the former is used as a metaphor for the latter. Many *khyāl, thumrī,* and *ghazal* texts are this way. A third category, less defined, includes all songs not in the above two categories, and may include many regional song styles relating to daily life, or film songs used in a dramatic or lighter contexts.

Devotional songs are among India's greatest genres, as has been suggested by the devotional component of this textbook. During the *Bhakti* era, and especially in its height in the fifteenth through the seventeenth centuries, countless singers and poets poured out their religious devotion in song. (The *Bhakti* period has a larger time span, but these centuries were the most productive from the standpoint of Hindustani song texts.) The names of Kabir, Surdas, Ramdas, Mirabai, Guru Nanak, and others are household names throughout north India, and their devotional poetry still often springs aloud from the heart and lips of young and old alike. There is no direct equivalent in the Christian tradition, for, although many can recite poetry and even passages of the Bible, there is no similar body of devotional literature which has so grasped the hold of the popular imagination as that of the *Bhakti* poets in India.

The Rajasthani poet Mirabai (1498–1547) is sometimes referred to as India's most renowned poet. In a land of such immense outpouring of verse, it would be impossible to say who is "greatest," but in terms of enduring and beloved popularity, she certainly stands alone. She was a beautiful young Rajput princess, who, as was the custom, was married by arrangement to a prince of a neighboring clan. It was a marriage of political convenience, and from the outset uncomfortable, for she considered herself the bride of Lord Krishna, the flute-playing, young elfin god who was the champion of the *Bhakti* period. When her husband died on the battlefield, Mirabai made a defiant domestic stance, openly rejecting the confines of widowhood in both dress and comportment. She danced and sang to Krishna and visited his shrines with the wandering saints and common people, outraging her noble in-laws with her public displays of devotion. After several unsuccessful attempts by her in-laws to kill her (she describes in verse that she was watched over by her Lord), she left the palace and wandered throughout northern India singing her poetry to Shyam, "the dark one," a name for Krishna. These poems speak to the poor and downtrodden, and hit on social conventions with a razor tongue. And yet, this poetry is marked with a devotional tenderness that has been set to song over and over again. It is not an intellectual body of poetry, but rather personal in its outpouring of ecstasy, with outrage at social injustice and mistreatment of women, all bathed in desire and torment over the separation between her and her Lord.

A SONG OF MIRABAI

Gone mad, sister,
my lover's departed, but listen—
a flute!
O whirling senses,

O heart reckless and tangled and mad!
What sort of flute
works this uncanny priest craft?
Even Mira's lord can't untangle this snare,
the power of seven musical notes.

translated by Andrew Schelling

The very popular light-classical singer Anup Jalota is loved for his renditions of devotional songs. In this recording on CD track 13, accompanied by harmonium, guitar, cymbals, and *tablā*, he sings one of Mira's bhajans, *Maine lino Govinda mol.*

Maine lino Govinda mol māyi ri
I have measured the worth Krishna, O my sister,

Koi kahe sasta, koi kahe mahenga
Some say cheap, others expensive,

Maine lino taraja tol . . .
I weighed him against pure gold.

Koi kahe chori, koi kahe sāni
Some say it's a secret, some say hidden,

Maine lino bajantā dhola . . .
I proclaim him out loud like a drum . . .

ACTIVITY 2.2 *On CD track 13, the artist wishes to convey the meaning of the text in an emphatic manner. Analyze and articulate the devices that both the poetess, Mirabai, and the singer, Anup Jalota, use to achieve this.*

In the second part of the excerpt, he comes across a word in old Rajasthani (dialect) that he feels his audience may not understand: sāni. He explains it, "chopa lena," which means "hidden away." Then he continues to sing. In your opinion, how does this affect the delivery of the song? Does it intrude on the music?

A MUSICIAN'S PRACTICE

The questions posed in Activity 2.1 raise the issue of how a musician brings feeling and life to the music. What is the bridge between the affect and the expression of it, and the transition from the conceptual to the world of the musical yogi?

"So, how is your practice coming?" So many times when classical musicians from India greet each other, this is an opening question— which is respectful, polite, and loving at the same time. And, in the typical absence of public recognition of younger musicians, the need for rededication is in constant need of a senior loving touch of encouragement. Since a musician is on a spiritual quest into sound, affect, technique, and composition, an inquiry into one's practice is at the same time intimate and endearing, and therefore encouraging. It is especially important when asked by older musicians of younger ones, for noticeable musical progress can seem to proceed at a snail's pace; frustration can be a regular companion.

When a musician practices, he or she sits down, and the word "sit" often substitutes for "practice." "Come sit with me," would be an invitation to a fellow student to come and practice a lesson together, or for an accompanist to join in. The word *riāz*, "practice," is used to describe the day-to-day sitting of a musician, in which the routines of exercises and scales, technique and literature are gone over and over, again and again, until they attain the kind of polish and luster which makes them presentable in concert. Musicians the world over know well this aspect of preparation. One says of a musician who has shown this polish that "he has *taiyārī*," which is like saying, "he is blooming, he is ripe, he is ready." One might also hear this in a negative sense: "He has learned much, but has no *taiyārī*"; or, "You know, it is very sad— he has such talent ("his hand is very good"), but he has not practiced and lost his *taiyārī*."

Years and years of *riāz* add up to *sādhanā*, which is "spiritual practice," and the word carries the additional senses of realization and fulfillment which are worthy of great respect. A younger musician might be praised for his *riāz*, in that he devotes long hours to honing his skills; but an older musician would be respected for his *sādhanā*, which would include his lifework in music—one who had spent many years teaching, performing, and in *riāz*.

A central figure in the shaping of the musician's experience is the teacher, or *guru*, a topic that is addressed in the next chapter. What a musician practices, how much he or she does it, its quality and inten-

sity, and how has it been shaped are all questions which have traditionally been in the hands of the teacher, whose presence is continually
felt throughout a musician's life. *Riāz, sādhanā*, and *guru* work to deepen
a musician's realization of the affect.

THE NINE MOODS

A musician spends years finding and shaping the *bhāva* or expression
of the *rāga*s. For the audience, the most tangible manifestation of affect
is hearing the musician build and bring out the mood of the *rāga*. Mood
is an essential part of the musical experience in India, and was discussed
in the earliest writings on music, especially in the seminal treatise, the
Natyasāstra, of the fourth century CE (the date of this and other treatises
are often disputed, since the original copies have long since disap-
peared). The treatise described eight primary moods, or *rasa*s (literally,
"juice," or "sap"), which were said to play an important role in drama,
dance, and music. Later, in the tenth century, a ninth *rasa* was added
to the list—peace—and hence the list is known as the "nine rasas," the
navaras.

Navaras—*the nine moods*
(pronounced "nuvvaruss")

karuna	sadness, pathos
shringār	love, joy
vira	heroism, valor
hāsya	laughter, comedy
raudra	anger
bhayānaka	fear
vibhātsa	digust
adbhuta	surprise
shānti	peace

In a dramatic performance (which includes classical dance), it is felt
that a judicious use of the first eight moods would leave the audience
with a feeling of the ninth, peace. In a musical performance, the first
four, and the ninth, find expression in the *rāga*s, or musical modes. The
moods of the other four, that is, anger, fear, disgust, and surprise, are
not regarded as inherent in the *rāga*s themselves, but rather can combine with stage action to create a greater dramatic effect.

There is a vast vocabulary to describe the shades of meaning of these moods. These descriptive words are called *bhāvas* ("expressions"), a word that is sometimes pronounced "*bhāo*" (rhymes with "cow"). *Bhāvas* are what artists spend years developing and refining, and are what communicates with and moves audiences. The *rasa shringār* ("love"), for instance, has so many *bhāvas:* happiness, joy, enchantment, wonder, ecstasy, infatuation, adoration, eroticism, devotion, and so on—there must be an infinite number of words to describe all the kinds of love.

In addition to the terminology of *rasa*, other terms are commonly used to describe the shades of feelings that can be conveyed by *rāgas*. *Rāgas* are roughly classified into two groups according to their nature: serious or light. A serious rāga is said to have *gambhīr prakrit* (serious nature). This might be said of the strictly classical literature in general. Lighter *rāgas* are said to have *chanchal prakrit* (restless nature). A *rāga* with a devotional tradition is described as having *bhakti ras* (devotional love), to distinguish it from the more romantic nature of *shringār ras*. Certain *rāgas* are said to have healing properties. But one must be careful in the casual dividing up of the literature, since the approach to a *rāga* may be very personalized by different artists, and one person's concept of "heavy" in music may be approached more lightly in another's version. Most musicians do not dwell on explaining all the possibilities of this terminology, but rather turn their attention directly to the sound of the music.

EXTRAMUSICAL EFFECTS

"Men are fools," my father said as we walked in the jungles behind our house. "They think only humans respond to beauty. But a feeding deer will drop its food to listen to music, and a king cobra sways its hood in pleasure. Listen. Do you hear that peacock's cry? It is the first note of the scale, **sa**."

It seemed to me that we were wandering only for pleasure. I did not realize that my father was teaching me the seven notes of the scale as described in the classic texts.

But at sunset we waited until the cowherds were driving their cattle back to their villages and my father said, "Can you hear that calf calling its mother? It is the note, **re**."

We watched my mother throwing vegetable peelings to the goats in our back field. "Hear the goats? If you sing **ga** three times, very quickly, it is the bleating of a goat."

We waded into the paddy fields behind the herons. "**Ma,** the cry of the heron."

At night, "**Pa,** the song of the nightingale."

In the bazaar streets as we followed the horse carriages, "**Dha,** the neighing of the horse."

And when the circus came to town, my father was excited at the opportunity of teaching me the last note of the scale. "Can you hear that **ni,** when the elephant trumpets?"

Gita Mehta, The Musician's Story, p. 204–5

This story has many versions—it has been told over and over for centuries. In the old classifications systems you will find the notes associated with birdcalls, animal sounds, colors, seasons, and planets. The difficulty is that no two writers seem to agree on which notes go with which particular natural phenomena—the note **pa**, for instance, may be described as the color gold in one place and blue in another. But the connection of the music with the natural world is vital to the musical lore. In the medieval period (the twelfth through the seventeenth centuries), the *rāg*s were thought of in terms of family and large clan relationships. There were parent and offspring *rāg*s, hence, male and female ones (*rāginīs*), once again with a confusingly disparate number of genealogies. Many of these family trees identified six main (male) *rāg*s, and each of these had six wives. Some of these would lists sons and grandsons. Often these would have a short poetic description of the fanciful qualities of the moods of the *rāg*s, such as this one about the male *rāg Hindol*, pictured in Figure 2.2.

A *RĀGAMĀLA* DESCRIPTION OF *RĀG HINDOL*

A lord is seated in a beautiful swing (hindol).
It is inlaid with gold
and covered with flowers and lotuses.
He is surrounded by women singing songs,
which delight the ear.

Painters would be commissioned to paint sets of miniature paintings of entire *rāg* families, called *rāgamālas*, which would then be bound in books and presented to their patrons. Many of these miniatures are among the most beautiful artistic treasures of the world. But art lovers are often disappointed that the modern musical traditions do not follow the imaginative flights of fancy of the medieval artists and poets.

However, one aspect of the extramusical qualities of *rāg* remains quite strong in Hindustani music: the association of time and season. Each *rāg* is assigned a place in the course of the day, according to eight three-hour time periods, roughly starting at midnight: four for late-night to noon, and four for afternoon to midnight.

FIGURE 2.2 *A* rāgamāla *painting* Rāg Hindol. *From the sixteenth through the nineteenth centuries, miniature paintings, often with stylistic influences from Persia and China, were in great vogue in the courts of North India.* Rāgamāla *paintings were collected in sets, with fanciful images of the* rāga, *often based on a poetic text.* Rāga Hindol *("swing") is a* rāga *of the springtime, and the dark sky of the painting suggests that cool relief from the hot weather is on the way. In depictions of this* rāga, *a lord (here the blue color identifies this as Lord Krishna) is seated on a swing surrounded by women who bring sweets and sing songs. Peacocks, one of the Krishna's symbols, are said to announce the coming of rain with their call.*

Sitārist Ravi Shankar described the sound of the ghats *(river steps) as follows:*

All the maharajahs had their mansion or palace on the bank of the river [Ganges], and many of them had their own shāhnai *(a type of oboe) player. These musicians had five or six duties per day—early morning, mid-morning, afternoon, early evening, evening, and night. Constantly one heard the beautiful* rāgas *of that particular hour, and altogether it created a music of its own. They blended so beautifully, into a harmony, really. That particular sound of the* ghāts *in Benaras was unique.*

Ravi Shankar, Rāgamāla

A principal factor in the mood of any time of day is the light. Since sunrise and sunset vary throughout the year and with the latitude, it not useful to assign the *rāgs* to times on the clock. Musicians might say, "This *rāg (Bairāgi)* is for when the sky is still gray in the morning, before the sun comes up"; or, "*Rāg Bhimpalāshri* is for the very late afternoon, when the sky is red, and all the animals are basking in the last sunshine"; or, "Play *Purvi* in the evening when you light the first lamp," and so on. There are a few *rāgs* which have seasonal implications (those of the spring and rainy seasons are especially important), and several which are appropriate to particular occasions, like the wedding rāg, *Shahāna*.

Most Hindustani musicians respect the traditional time classifications of the *rāgas*. But in these days of recording sessions scheduled at all hours, restricted practice schedules because of work commitments, and fixed evening concert times, the rigidity of the timing is relaxing quite a bit. A few musicians have abandoned it altogether as a romantic fancy of the past with little bearing on their own practice or performance.

CONCLUSION

In this chapter, affect has been associated with the "meaningless" expression of the syllable, as it is used in recitation of Vedic texts, *dhrupad* style, and in the vocal genre known as *tarānā*. The musician's practice was looked at briefly as a window on how he works to bring out the expression in the *rāgas*. Affect and mood were also discussed as part of the ancient classification systems of *rāga* according to the *navaras* and the older systems of associating the ragas with natural phenomena, culminating with the *rāgamāla* genre of painting.

CHAPTER 3

Teaching, Learning, and Performing Music

In 1924, the art historian Ananda Coomaraswamy wrote a short essay on the classical music of India in which he noted:

> As in other arts and in life, so here also India presents us to the wonderful spectacle of the still-surviving consciousness of the ancient world, with a range of emotional experience rarely accessible to those who are preoccupied with the activities of overproduction, and intimidated by the economic insecurity of a social order based on competition.
>
> The art music of India exists only under cultivated patronage, in its own intimate environment. It corresponds to all that is most classical in the European tradition. It is the chamber music of an aristocratic society, where the patron retains musicians for his own entertainment and for the pleasure of the circle of his friends; or it is temple music, where the musician is the servant of God. The public concert is unknown, and the livelihood of the artist does not depend upon his ability and will to amuse the crowd. In other words, the musician is protected. Under these circumstances he is under no temptation to be anything but a musician; his education begins in infancy, and his art remains a vocation. The civilizations of Asia do not afford to the inefficient amateur those opportunities of self-expression, which are so highly appreciated in Europe and in America. The arts are nowhere taught as a social accomplishment; on the one hand, there is the professional, proficient in a traditional art, and on the other the lay public. The musical cultivation of the public does not consist in "everybody doing it," but in appreciation and reverence. (*The Dance of Shiva and Other Essays*, 72–73)

How quickly things change! In 1947 India declared her independence, and the life of the music and musicians began to undergo many radical changes. The old feudal system, with its maharajas and nawabs, courts and refined society, began to disappear in favor of a new democracy—one in which the classical musician was no longer the employee of a privileged society, nor protected from the economics of competition. He became dependent for his livelihood on the more recent social developments, namely the public concert, and eventually in the electronic media: film, radio, TV, and recording. These opened up to a spectacular new horizon for the musician: the world beyond India. As we enter the twenty-first century, we are rapidly losing the magic of the more secluded world described by Coomaraswamy, and opening into a realm of conscious reinterpretation of the ancient values he prized. The physical presence of the music teacher continues, nevertheless, to be of prime importance.

Guru kripya bina koi nahi pave—*without the blessings of the guru, one gets nothing.*

Well-worn old song text

TEACHING AND LEARNING MUSIC

A central figure in the old system was the *guru* (literally, simply "teacher," but often interpreted in the sense of *sādguru*, "merciful and worthy preceptor—the one who removes arrogance"). In a more or less closed musical society, one's guru was arranged in one's early, formative years, and continued to be a decisive figure throughout a lifetime. A student's connection to the music was through the guru, since there were no other media from which one could learn—and one did not divide one's attention among several gurus. The guru was a dynamic figure, conducting the daily regimen of practice and learning, and regulating all facets of the musical growth of the disciple (*shishya*). The student's attitude, conceptions, and technical prowess was both the product and responsibility of the guru, and it was a relationship not to be taken lightly, since it involved a great commitment on both sides. A student lived with or near the guru and attended to the needs of the rhythm of his/her household—shopping, cleaning, cooking, and serving whenever called upon. In a ceremony early in the relationship, a thread was tied around the wrist of the student, symbolically binding him or her into a permanent relationship. The student was usually financially dependent on the guru as well, so the student was not free to come and go at will. The music, of course, was the bond, and assumed a role as language of communication, devotion, and profession. The guru taught the music directly through oral repetition: hear, repeat, practice, repeat, hear again, practice. A literature of *rāg* and *tāl* was accumulated slowly along with the technical abilities to be executed with greater and greater refinement and discernment of ear, and the student was continually required to prove that he or she was ready for the next step. The guru's repertoire was often a highly guarded treasure, and not simply distributed at the behest of the student. In this centuries-old economic system, the guru was a master in a professional guild, and admission to it was an economic guarantee of a livelihood in music. Therefore, in this rarefied atmosphere that protected the musical lineage, as well as the professional world to which it led, to get a new composition was an honor bestowed upon the student. The years of slowly measured progress and refinement developed attitudes of patience, respect, and humility in the student. This is readily apparent in the music.

What is a guru? I recently heard an old pakhāwaj player put it this way: "A guru gives blood."

Kathak dancemaster Chitresh Das

There are other changes in style that come with the modern world of the classical musician. In a recent discussion with sarod-master Ali Akbar Khan, he remarked:

> In my younger days, I got a chance to hear many great musicians in court and at the music festivals. At that time, there were two styles of music: *dhrupad* and *khyāl* styles. In our style, that my father learned from Wazir Khansahib [of the court of Rampur], it was dhrupad, and nowadays you don't hear that old style. Of course, my father brought many parts together, so that you could play the many different sections of vocal and instrumental music all on one instrument like on the sarod and sitar. You could then complete all the sections of ālāp— all fifteen sections—which you could not do on the old instruments, or just with voice alone. Now people have started changing those styles, and they don't know how to start and how to end. Nowadays in what you hear, the sections are not fully done. You hear a mix of a little from here, a little from there, and often they mess it up.

Modern approaches to learning music suggest a different approach to the old traditions. If a student pays his teacher for regular lessons, the economic power resides in the hands of the student, and he can withdraw this at any time according to whether he is pleased with what he is getting. Under these circumstances, the teacher has to please the student to avoid frustration with progress, or suffer negative reactions to his own criticisms about tempo, style, and choice of materials. Despite what the student states about the ideals of dedication to the guru, he will nevertheless retain control. On his own, he will seek out books on the music, printed versions of the literature, and recorded versions of the *rāgs* being learned. His freedom to spend extended time with the teacher may be reduced to one lesson a week, and more hours may be spent with recorded music. There are great benefits in such a modified system, but they will not add up to the same style of training as the old *guru-shishyā paramparā* (teacher-disciple tradition).

The teacher is of a musical family implied by the guru-as-the-father (or mother) and is called a *gharānā* (from *ghar*, "house"). Another word, *khandan* ("family", "clan") is also heard, but it refers more to the bloodlines and intermarriages of musical families. The *gharānā* system also includes the inherited musical style of a teacher including the selection of *rāgs*, and compositions within them, as well as the choices of how to expand the *rāg* in performance (which will be covered in Chapter 5). The *gharānā* system was especially powerful in the old days of aristocratic patronage, where geographic centrality in a gharānā was implicit. We know of many of these gharānās by their court names: Gwalior gharānā, Lucknow, Patiala, Rampur, Maihar, and so on. Others are known by the founding personalities or place of origin: Alladiya Khan (a *khyāl* singer) gharānā, Imdad (a *sitār/surbahār* player) Khan gharānā, Kirana (a village) gharānā, and so on. If the old sense of the term gharānā is becoming more diffuse in contemporary centers of urban musical activity, the idea still plays an important part in a musician's life and music, since the bulk of his training will have come through a single guru. He may acknowledge that a given composition he plays is from another gharānā, but he will still render it within the style he learned, using ornaments and expansions particular to his own training.

The changes in the old order have affected the study in other ways. A teacher may organize a musical sitting once or twice a day for morning and evening sessions with his or her students. Included among these may be old and long-time students as well as newcomers. Most of these will not have professional musical aspirations. They may hold other jobs in the community, or may be using the classical musical lessons to provide variety and depth to other musical concentrations: from jazz and pop music to musicology. The idea of music as a refinement for the young is pursued by many parents anxious to provide opportunities and polish to their offspring, much like taking piano lessons. Prior to modern urbanized India, these would have been social graces and refinements available for the princely families alone.

Of course, many of the musical changes have come about as the musicians struggle for economic and artistic survival. An artist must often spend long weeks on the road, and does not have the leisure to sit with students regularly. Ali Akbar Khan continued:

> At the time of the courts, the musicians didn't have to think always about travel and money matters, they could think more about the music. They might have only a few disciples to train in a proper way.

FIGURE 3.1   *Ali Akbar Khan and Zakir Hussain in concert in California in the 1970s. The* sarod *and the* tablā *are accompanied by a droning* tānpurā, *played by Susan Rosenbloom. In the front row of the audience are flutist G. S. Sachdev, vocalist Marilyn Spencer, and sarodists George Ruckert and Ross Kent. Judging from the expressions, it is a moment of deep concentration.*   (Photo courtesy Betsey Bruner.)

And, when they had to perform in court, they had to do the right things, because the rulers often had a great knowledge of music, so nobody dared to play games with money business; they only cared about the music.

Nowadays, the younger generation doesn't think about the purity of the *rāgas*—even they don't follow the time: they sing morning *rāgas* in the evening or anytime. These kinds of changes are coming, but it is not good for the music, and it is not good for the listeners, and it's not good for your health. Because this sound is created by God, and it was passed down through the *rishis* (saints) to help [mankind] purify the mind and soul. Then you can think about love and not about ego, image, or that kind of thing.

OLD TRADITIONS IN NEW PACKAGES

Some of the greatest influences in the worldview of modern Indian music have been the concerts and recordings of *sitārist* Ravi Shankar. Ravi-ji, as he is affectionately and respectfully addressed, had extensive contact with audiences beyond India as a youth in his brother Uday Shankar's dance troupe. He was the ideal musical ambassador of his time. Blessed with a phenomenal technique, a fine ear, a gift for composition, and a thorough grounding in the tradition from his teacher, Allauddin Khan, he strode like a giant across the world stage during the 1950s through the 1990s. This was at a time when a hunger for the musical gifts that India could offer was whetted by the popular endorsement of the Beatles and the many spiritual gurus who were opening the world to the East—to say nothing of the worldwide expansion in marketing of Japanese, American, and European goods and ideas. His programs were always exciting and fast-paced, and introduced the music to many who were hearing it presented for the first time in a very palatable and highly polished format.

"You must understand," said the distinguished modern *tablā* player Zakir Hussain in a recent interview, "that the classical music has had to become a performance art form. In former times it was limited to the palaces and some occasional festivals. But it has emerged as an entertainment idiom, and that has necessitated changes in its packaging. Today's musician is more aware of his or her audience and the aesthetics—careful attention is being paid to the audience. Not taxing them. Giving them more variety. More different items in a program presenting a wider view of the moods and styles. And the shift has been from vocal music, which was the centerpiece in the past, to instrumental music—this has been done by Ali Akbar Khan (sarodist) and Ravi Shankar (sitārist).

In part of what Zakir-ji calls the "packaging" of the music, one hears a different concert now than in former days. In the early part of the twentieth century, a program might last for four to five hours and would include two or three *rāgs*. Now, performances are usually in the three-hour range, and may well have as many as six or more items, especially in vocal concerts, when several short songs are presented toward the end of a recital. The microphone has changed the delivery of both voice and instrument, and the subtlety of ornamentation and refinement of dynamic control is more highly defined. What the older musicians decry as a lack of stamina, the younger ones laud as an increase in the communicative power.

"Consider the old compositions and those older artists: they were all playing in *tīntāl* (the sixteen-beat rhythm cycle, which has some relationship to 4/4 time in the West)," Zakir-ji continues. "It's quite different nowadays. Now you hear many more *tāls* in concert. I consider it a challenge to make eleven-beat cycles approachable to the audience! I wouldn't call that a watering-down of the music. I hear new *rāgas* all the time, many that I never heard the names of when I was growing up. And the playing is on a high level, too. I think there are more excellent *tablā* players today than ever before, and they are doing great new things with the *tablā*!

In this chapter we have not dealt with the syllable, but rather the devotional component of the music that is very much alive in the *guru-shishyā* tradition, even if the modern performances have become a bit more like modern concerts the world over: shorter with an emphasis on variety and innovation. And perhaps the fixed-improvisation thread can be best seen here with the fixity of an older style of presentation of the music improvising to adapt to the new conditions of the modern concert hall.

CHAPTER 4

Rhythm and Drumming

There are two basic ways of thinking about the rhythmic element in Indian classical music: that which is free—has no meter at all, and that which is definitely metric. These are called *anibaddh-nibaddh*, "unbound and bound." *Ālāp*, the primary *anibaddh* format for Hindustani music, will be discussed in Chapter 6. The music that is in a metric cycle, or *tāl* (Sanskrit *tāla*), is termed *nibaddh*.

The rhythms all come from speech patterns, which were made into poetic meters, and then classified according to types. These became spoken as abstract syllables, grouped into types containing short (given a count of 1) and long (given a count of 2) syllables, and were given specific names, like magana *(2 + 2 + 2),* jagana *(1 + 2 + 1),* yagana *(1 + 2 + 2), and so on. These became the sections of the* tāl *system. You can see, then, that these poetic meters were the systematic combination of long and short vowel sounds, which in turn was translated into rhythmic language.*

Swapan Chaudhuri

Listening to the short recitation of syllables on CD track 14 will introduce you to the "rhythmic language" that tablā master Swapan Chaudhuri (see Figure 4.1) refers to in the citation above. The selection is made up of compositions taken from *Kathak* dance and *tablā* drumming, recited here by dancer Joanna Das and percussionist Ritesh Das of the Toronto Tablā Ensemble. The lyrical and exciting patter of this recitation demonstrates the felicity and variety of rhythms, words, and sounds found in this rich rhythmic vocabulary.

FIGURE 4.1 *Swapan Chaudhuri playing the* tablā.

The classification of poetic meters that Swapan-ji refers to brings up a wonderful old word: *yamātārājabhānasalagām.* The short a's have an "uh" sound, as in the word "but"; the long ā's are protracted, as in "father." Say it aloud: *ya-mā-tā-rā-ja-bhā-na-sa-la-gām.* It does not have meaning, but was used as a mnemonic device to remember the different meters of classical Sanskrit poetry, something akin to what the ancient Greeks and later European poets thought of as *iambs, dactyls, anapests,* and so on.

ya-mā	short-long (iamb)
ya-mā-tā	short-long-long (bacchius)
sa-la-gām	short-short-long (anapest)
tā-rā-ja	long-long-short (dactyl)
. . . and so on.	

TĀLA

Ancient rhythmic theory divided the longer cycles of beats into groups of short (*laghu*) and long sections. These groups were strung together to make the rhythmic cycles known as *tāla*s. The divisions were marked by hand gestures, namely, claps and waves of the hand. For example, *tīntāl* (literally, "three claps"), the most common *tāla* today, is a cycle of four groups of four beats, marked by three claps and a wave in the following order: clap-clap-wave-clap. The groups are shown with vertical bars in the following diagram, and the numbers refer to the beats. Clap (or wave) on the first of each group of four:

```
clap            clap           wave             clap
 1   2   3   4 | 5   6   7   8 | 9   10   11   12 | 13   14   15   16
```

The claps that signify the divisions of the rhythmic cycle are assigned numbers; waves (some *tāl*s haves more than one) are all called *khālī* ("empty"), and are marked with a zero. Since the first beat of any cycle is most important, it has a special name called the *sam* (pronounced "sum") and it is marked with a plus sign instead of a "1." So tīntāl is notated with the numbers like this:

```
+ (clap)      2 (clap)       0 (wave)         3 (clap)
 1   2   3   4 | 5   6   7   8 | 9   10   11   12 | 13   14   15   16
```

THEKĀ: THE TĀL AS A SUCCESSION
OF DRUM SOUNDS

Indian musicians substitute the syllable again for the numbers. They relate to the *tāl*s through their commonly known drum strokes, which have syllabic names. The pattern of drum syllables which is the "signature" for *tīntāl* is:

+ (clap)				2 (clap)				0 (wave)				3 (clap)			
dha	dhin	dhin	dha	dha	dhin	dhin	dha	dha	tin	tin	ta	ta	dhin	dhin	dha
1	2	3	4	5	6	7	8	9	10	11	12	13	14	15	16

Note that the beats 10 through 13 have "t-" beginnings, while all the rest have "dh-" initial consonants. Furthermore, this dh- to t- change is slightly off the foursquare pattern of the *tāl*'s structure. It is a peculiarity of this *tāl* to be structured so, and gives it a great dynamic lift in its sound. On the *tablā*, which is a combination of a left and a right hand drum (Figure 4.1), the "t-" sounds are produced with the right hand alone striking its drum, while the "dh-" sounds are produced by both drums striking simultaneously: a treble and bass sound together.

This signature pattern of drum syllables is known as the *thekā* (pronounced "tay-kāh"). Musicians know the various *tāls* by their *thekās*. Some of the common *thekās* that all classical musicians know are shown below:

Dādra tāl (6 beats, 3 + 3)
```
+            0
Dhi dhi na | dha tun na
```

Rupak tāl (7 beats, 3 + 2 + 2) This one is unique in that the first beat is a wave.
```
0           1          2
tin tin na | dhin na | dhin na
```

Kehārwā tāl (8 beats, 4 + 4)
```
+            0
Dha ge na ti | na ka dhi na
```

Jhaptāl (10 beats, 2 + 3 + 2 + 3)
```
+       2         0      3
Dhi na | dhi dhi na | ti na | dhi dhi na
```

Chautāl (12 beats, 2 + 2 + 2 + 2 + 2 + 2)
```
+          0        2           0        3          4
Dha dha | dhin ta | kat dhage | dhin ta | tete kata | gadi gena
```

Dhamār tāl (14 beats 5 + 2 + 3 + 4)
```
+                   2       0        3
Kat dhe te dhe te | dha — | ge te te | te te ta —
```

Sitarkhāni tāl (16 beats, 4 + 4 + 4 + 4)
+   2
Dha gadhi -ga dha | dha gadhi -ga dha |
0   3
dha kati -ka ta | ta gadhi -ga dha

Keep in mind that rhythmic theory in Hindustani music is imbedded in all genres of classical music; it is not only for drummers. All musicians use the drum syllables to learn and communicate the different categories of rhythm and their variations. Musicians who do not play the drums can often recite many intricate percussion patterns, as well as the *thekā*s listed.

COUNTING PATTERNS IN *TĀL*

Teachers are likely to give their students counting patterns (*gintī* exercises) which teach the essentials of maintaining the rhythm and the *tāl*. CD Tracks 15–17 demonstrate some *gintī* patterns in *tīntāl*, and Activity 4.1 will guide you through them. I recommend that you try to do the exercises without looking at the page. Hearing the examples on the recording is easier than seeing all the numbers, but you can see how it works in the following charts.

ACTIVITY 4.1   Gintī *exercises in* tīntāl
When performing these exercises, clap the tāl *at a medium speed, and recite the numbers as directed.*

CD track 15. In this exercise, the numbers progress consecutively— ascending and descending from 1 to 9 then 1-8-1-7-1-6-1-5, and so on, and progress up again. The tension in the rhythm comes from your clapping pattern running contrary to your recitation pattern until the very last beat, at which there should be a triumphal resolution!

+   2   0   3   +   2   0   3
1 2 3 4 | 5 6 7 8 | 9 8 7 6 | 5 4 3 2 | 1 2 3 4 | 5 6 7 8 | 7 6 5 4 | 3 2 1 2

+   2   0   3   +   2   0   3
3 4 5 6 | 7 6 5 4 | 3 2 1 2 | 3 4 5 6 | 5 4 3 2 | 1 2 3 4 | 5 4 3 2 | 1 2 3 4

```
+      2      0      3      +      2      0      3
3 2 1 2 | 3 2 1 2 | 1 2 1 2 | 3 2 1 2 | 3 4 3 2 | 1 2 3 4 | 5 4 3 2 | 1 2 3 4

+      2      0      3      +      2      0      3
5 6 5 4 | 3 2 1 2 | 3 4 5 6 | 7 6 5 4 | 3 2 1 2 | 3 4 5 6 | 7 8 7 6 | 5 4 3 2

+      2      0      3      +
1 2 3 4 | 5 6 7 8 | 9 8 7 6 | 5 4 3 2 | 1
```

CD track 16. This *gintī* exercise groups the beats in threes (two numbers plus one rest), again in a sequence of 9-8-7-6-, and so on.

```
+      2      0      3      +      2      0      3
9 8–7 | 6–5 4 | –3 2–| 1 8–7 | 6–5 4 | –3 2–| 1 7–6 | 5–4 3

+      2      0      3      +      2      0      3      +
–2 1 –| 6 5 – 4 | 3 – 2 1 | – 5 4 – | 3 2 – 1 | 4 – 3 2 | – 1 3 – | 2 1 – 2 | 1
```

CD track 17. This *gintī* is one that tests your ability to hold the beat while you recite on and off the beat, again with the 9-8-7-, sequence. Notice that the odd numbered sequences are on the beat and the even ones off the beat.

```
+      2      0      3      +      2      0      3
1 – 2 – | 3 – 4 – | 5 – 6 – | 7 – 8 – | 9 1 – 2 | – 3 – 4 | – 5 – 6 | – 7 – 8

+      2      0      3      +      2      0      3
1 – 2 – | 3 – 4 – | 5 – 6 – | 7 1 – 2 | – 3 – 4 | – 5 – 6 | 1 – 2 – | 3 – 4 –

+      2      0      3      +
5 1 – 2 | – 3 – 4 | 1 – 2 – | 3 1 – 2 | 1
```

THE *TABLĀ*

The primary drum in North India is the paired set known collectively as *tablā* ("tub-luh"). More precisely, the right-hand drum is the *tablā*, and the left-hand one the *bāyā* ("left"). Their origin and early development in India is a bit unclear, but most scholars maintain that it was descended from a West Asian drum pair called the *tabl* which came into India with the Persian and Arabic musical influences of the Middle Ages. Another fanciful story tells of their origin through an incident on an eighteenth century stage:

> The *pakhāwaj* is a double-headed, barrel-shaped drum, which has a smaller treble and a larger bass end, played by the right and left hands

respectively. Two famous *pakhāwaj* players were having a contest, the loser of which was to have his drum split in half—a humiliating defeat. The losing player, traditionally suggested to have been Sidhar Khan of Delhi, took his split drum home, stood the two parts upright, and played them as separate drums. *"Tab bhi bolā*— "Still it speaks!" said onlookers in surprise.

Sidhar Khan is considered to be the founder of the Delhi *gharānā*, the oldest of the six *tablā* traditions.

However fanciful, this story suggests the era that the *tablā* began to assume its important role in the music—in the time of Sidhar Khan (eighteenth century Delhi)—and the fact that drummers played the compositions and style of the elder classical drum, the *pakhāwaj*. The success of the *tablā* came as a result of two qualities it possesses: first, it can easily imitate the style of a number of drums, from the dignified *pakhāwaj* and courtly *naqqara*, to the lively and expressive *dhol, nāl*, and other folk drums. And second, it can show the contrast between open and closed sounds of the bass drum, which allows the sounds of *thekā*s and other types of compositions to be easily grasped by the listener. The older style of maintaining the *tāl* with hand gestures, which often required a separate person assigned to do only that, took a second place to this vital and versatile pair of drums.

KĀYDĀ

A *kāydā* (or *qāydā*, literally "rule, law") is a composition which takes advantage of the *tablā*'s ability to contrast open and closed sounds. It is a theme-and-variations genre of composition in which a given composition (the *kāydā)* is put through a series of regulated permutations. In the *kāydā* in Figure 4.2, notice how there is a rough symmetry between the first lines of the composition (with dh- sounds) and its mirroring second part (with t- sounds).

TIHĀĪ

The *tihāī* ("one-third") is one of the most common rhythmic formulas in the music. When a rhythmic or melodic phrase is repeated three times, it is called a *tihāī*. A *tihāī* is usually a concluding figure that brings a section to a close but can also be composed to be played as an independent composition. Most often the *tihāī* is calculated to

Delhi Kayda (qayda)
theme and variations form for tabla

theme

+

dha te te dha te te dha dha | ²te te dha ge tu na ke na

⁰ta te te ta te te dha dha | ³te te dha ge dhi na ge na

variation 1

+

[dha te te dha te te dha dha] 2x, 1st line

[ta te te ta te te ta ta] 2x, 1st line with dhi na ge na

variation 2

+

[dha te te dha te te] 2x, dha dha te te, 1st line

[ta te te ta te te] 2x, dha dha te te, 1st line with dhi na ge na

variation 3

+

[te te dha te te dha] 2x, te te dha dha, 1st line

[te te ta te te ta] 2x, te te dha dha, 1st line with dhi na ge na

tihai

+

[dha te te dha te te dha dha te te dha ge dhi na ge na

dha te dha dha dha ⁽⁺⁾—] 3x

FIGURE 4.2 *Delhi Kāydā.*

end on the downbeat, but sometimes they are tailored to come to the beginning of the composition (since not all compositions start on *sam*). Figure 4.3, and CD tracks 18–22 illustrate a series of *tihāī's* which have been composed on the drumming phrase, *te te ka ta ga di ge na*. It is helpful if you say this phrase over and over a number of times, so that it rolls off your tongue. The plus mark in parentheses indicates that the final *dha* comes out on the *sam*.

Tihāīs using tete kata gadi gena
Clap tintāl and say the following patterns.

+   (+)

CD track 18. [tete kata gadi gena dha —] 3×

+   (+)

CD track 19. [(tete kata gadi gena dha) 3× — —] 3×

+   (+)

CD track 20. [te te – ka ta – tete kata gadi gena dha] 3×

+

CD track 21. [te – te ka – ta ga – di ge – na dha

                                 (+)

te te ka ta ga di ge na dha tete kata gadi gena dha] 3×

CD track 22. This is a derivative composition with a
tihāī at the end, called a *tukra.*

+

dha — gena dha — gadi gena dha — kata gadi gena
dha

                     (+)

— [tete kata gadi gena dha — —] 3×

FIGURE 4.3   Tihāīs *with* tete kata gadi gena

CD track 23 contains a *chakradār tihāī* first recited, then played on the *tablā* by two of the greatest tablā contemporary virtuosos: the late Ustad Alla Rakha and his brilliant son, Zakir Hussain (Figure 4.4). A *chakradār* is a composition ending in a *tihāī* that is itself played three times: hence the *tihāī* portion of the composition is heard nine times in all. They recite the composition in alternation: first Alla Rakha-ji begins, followed by Zakir-ji, then both together (which is how they play it just after they recite). Alla Rakha-ji states after the recitation that it is a composition of his *guru,* the late Kadir Baksh of Lahore, Pakistan. You will note that the performers sometimes change the syllables as they recite, but this is done only for sound and accent— the strokes are essentially the same.

At the 2″ mark of CD track 23 comes a *tipallī gat* composition: a drum composition in which three identical parts are recited at three different speeds: duple-triple-fast duple. The remarkable aspect of these compositions is that they work out in *tāl.* The first section is in twos (or fours, if you think of it as written in Figure 4.5), the second in threes (or sixes), and the last section is in fours (or eights). As in the

FIGURE 4.4 Tabla *master Zakir Hussain in concert. Zakir-ji appears to be counting a rhythmic pattern with the fingers of his left hand, which is a way of keeping track of the beats and* tāls *in the complicated cross rhythms such as those found in* tihāīs *and* gintī *patterns.* (Photo courtesy of Susana Millman.)

+_____ , _____ ,
[Dha—na dha ki ta dha tre kre dhet te te te te kre
2
te te ka ta ga di ge na dha — ka ta dha —' dha -na
0
dhakita dhatrekre dhetete tetekre dhetete kataga digena dha- ka
3
tadha-' dha-nadha kitadhatrekredhetete tetekredhetetekata
+
gadigena dha-kata dha'

FIGURE 4.5 Tipallī chakradār.

first *chakradār*, Alla Rakha recites first, then Zakir Hussain, then both recite together. You will have to listen carefully: it goes by very quickly.

OTHER DRUMMING TRADITIONS

If you follow the legends, you can trace the language of the tablā back to the rhythmic art of the great Lord Shiva. The little drum on which he played is called a damaru [waisted-shaped drum]. And when he played at medium speed it sounded like "diga diga diga." When it went fast, it sounded like "taka taka taka." That is the first sound of all the drums, and also the basic sound of the footwork in the dance.

Zakir Hussain

From the earliest drums made out of holes in the ground covered with animal hides, to the ceremonial and war drums of antiquity, to contemporary India's sophisticated *mridangam, pakhāwaj,* and *tablā,* the drums reflect a cultural romance with the technique and sound of drumming of every conceivable type. Drums inspire religious assemblies, announce royalty, and fire up armies for battle. It is hard to think of an ensemble without a drum, from folk and pop to classical. As solo instruments, they are played with a revealing virtuosity and compositional imagination unrivaled in the world.

Folk drumming is often highly complex, even though it is usually based on short duple and triple meters. There are many regional folk drums, a few of which are played with sticks, but most are hand drums. The *dholak,* or its regional variant, the *dhol,* is a double-ended drum that is identifiable by its lilting bass sound. In the Punjab, *dhol* refers to a large cylindrical double-headed drum that the player hangs by a cord around his neck and shoulders. He may often dance while he plays, with hand and stick, the rousing rhythms of *bhangrā,* the Punjabi harvest dance that is now an international dance-club phenomenon. In most folk drumming, the patterns are repetitive, and the lilt, or "groove," of the drumming is highly desirable. This groove is a fundamental part of the light-classical tradition, and many of the very best drummers who can lay down a lively groove are engaged in the industry of producing film and pop music. It can be easier in this commercial sphere to make a living in the highly competitive world of Indian drumming.

The *pakhāwaj* is a classical drum associated with the *dhrupad* tradition (refer back to CD tracks 7–11). Like many other Indian drums, the right hand plays a smaller (treble) head, and the left—the larger—produces a lower sound. Since the sound travels back and forth within the barrel-shaped chamber, there is not a great pitch distinction between the overall sound of each hand. The construction of each drum head is different, and the right-end head is constructed of layers of goatskin, upon which is affixed a black multi-layered center spot made out of iron filings and rice paste. This gives the right-hand end a handful of ringing sounds that the drummer uses to his advantage to create variety and contrast in his timbres. The left head is played with a temporary moistened lump of flour dough that adds bass resonance.

The *pakhāwaj* bequeaths a huge repertory of playing technique and compositional styles to the *tablā*. For the last one hundred years, the *tablā* has assumed its position as the preeminent classical drum. Furthermore, players of lighter music favor it as well. The reason for this is the versatility of these paired drums: the players can both produce the lilting rhythmic grooves of the light music, as well as play the poetic compositions of the classical drums in styles ranging from fiery to delicate. They can hold their own in accompanying the *sitār* and *sarod*, the dance, vocal music, and the myriad of ensemble pieces in which they usually play an active role.

CONCLUSION

This chapter has featured two of the three threads that you are following through this book. The verbal syllables were those of drumming, by which artists learn and communicate the complexities of North Indian meter and rhythm. The fixed compositions featured on the accompanying CD can be effectively recited and played. The next chapter turns to melody.

CHAPTER 5

Song and Performance

I know not how thou singest, my master!
I ever listen in silent amazement.
The light of thy music illumines the world.
The life breath of thy music
runs from sky to sky.
The holy stream of thy music breaks through
all stony obstacles and rushes on.
My heart longs to join in thy song,
but vainly struggles for a voice.
I would speak, but speech breaks not into song,
and I cry out baffled.
Ah, thou hast made my heart captive
in the endless meshes of thy music, my master!

Rabindranath Tagore, Gitanjali

To both the insider and outsider, India has long been a land of beguiling melody and song. More than one listener, caught in its allure and appeal, has echoed the words of the thirteenth-century West Asian musician, Amir Khusrau, who said, "Indian music, the fire that burns heart and soul . . . charms not only men, but the animals are transfixed also." It is not only (to some) "the curious and exotic tonalities"—there is something in the soulful comprehensiveness of the ancient airs that suggests an approach to music as a whole which is on the one hand romantic and fanciful, and realistic, imaginative, and confident on the other. The long path of this music is well trodden.

COMPOSITION AND IMPROVISATION

What is a song? Succinctly, several lines of melody tied together by a few lines of text. There have been millions of songs in India's history, and she continues to pour them out in every style, from religious chanting to classical solos, to film songs and pop dance tunes—slow and fast, devotional and heroic, happy and sad. The classification of the songs into melodic types has yielded the concept of *rāga*, one of the great legacies of the music of the world. The central feature of a *rāg* performance involves taking a fixed composition, such as a song, and elaborating it with ornamentation, expansions, and improvised additions.

However, the idea of improvisation is elusive and somewhat deceptive in Hindustani classical music. Those who relate to the word "improvisation" in its jazz sense of reworking melodic patterns over a chordal harmony do not instantly grasp the compositional restrictions and elaborations suggested to the musician who plays or sings a *rāg*. For the latter musician, it is largely a question of selecting a few notes and phrases, and then placing these melodic phrases into a balance suggested by the traditions of the *rāg* and the school (*gharānā*) of its performer.

The methods of achieving these balances are absorbed through the hours spent with a teacher, who leads the student through hundreds of models of the *rāg* in both composition and on-the-spot expansion. Repeating a phrase back according to the teacher's approval is the only way the tradition manifests its "correctness." A young performer is likely to render a *rāg* with very strict accord to what he was taught— almost like a rote repetition of a composition in the sense of strictly playing a Mozart sonata or Chopin etude. Those who have studied a bit longer will start to take liberties with the timing, ornamentation, and even the ordering of the phrases. A mature musician will do this with a freedom and control that suggests complete spontaneity, inventing new patterns as he represents old ones. But all performers start from a similar point of departure: "This is the way my teacher showed me how to do it."

A fixed composition in a *rāg*, whether a song (usually in Hindi) or an instrumental melody, is called a *bandish*. A musician who can sing or play a number of these is highly respected. One musician recently praised the late Jnan Ghosh of Calcutta, saying, "You know, Jnan-da (pronounced "gyan-da": -da is a suffix denoting an elder brother) knew so many—sooo many—compositions from this *gharānā*, that *gharānā*, in vocal music and *tablā*, and he taught them to so many students—oof!— you will not see his like ever again." Often when musicians lament the passing of one of the older generation, they describe it, apart from the personal endearments, as a loss in terms of the many compositions that the person knew.

The fixed compositions carry the maps of the *rāgs*—the balances of the notes, the moods, the typical phrases, the proper way to begin and end—in short, the lore of the *rāgs*. Some of this lore has been fairly recently written in modern books devoted to *rāga*, but the essential factor in bearing the tradition along from one generation to the next is the <u>sound</u> of these compositions, functioning as models for rendering the *rāg*.

> *A composition is like a snapshot, you see. Like you go to your friend's house and see an album of the family pictures. From one picture of this cousin you get some idea of how he looks. But then you see many pictures of him and you start to get a real idea of that person. Like that you learn the picture of the* rāg.
> *But still you won't know it until you practice and play it. Even now I am still learning about the* rāgs *every time I play.*
>
> Ali Akbar Khan

Certain vocal schools, such as the Gwalior *gharānā*, are known for their compositions, and the singers are likely to present them with some degree of pride in their performances, with meticulous attention to their detail of wording and phrasing. Artists from other schools might focus instead on the ornamentation or display imagination creating permutations of a composition. These elaborations of an original composition will still be considered rendering the "fixed" composition, but to nonaccustomed ears it might sound rather free. Still others will use the composition only as a quick springboard to the *rāg*'s more abstract elaborations, preferring to emphasize mood, technique, or other aspects of the *rāg*'s structure.

CD track 24 is a *bandish* in the afternoon *rāg*, *Gaur Sārang*, the first line of which is written in Figure 5.1. Like most compositions, it is in two parts, called *asthāī* (or *sthāyī*) and *antarā*. Some compositions may have more sections, or occasionally only one section. The *asthāī* will normally show the structure of the *rāg* in its home register, whereas the *antarā* (at the 54″ mark) will continue to the higher **sa** and above.

In CD track 24 Asha Bhosle sings a medium-tempo *khyāl* composition, *Bolo re papīha*, by Allauddin Khan (Figure 5.1). The words tell

The asthai begins

$$\text{G} \mid \overset{3}{\text{R}} \text{ S } - \overset{\frown}{\text{PMDP}} \mid \overset{+}{\text{m}} - \text{ G m} \mid \overset{2}{\text{G R mG Pm}} \mid \overset{0}{\text{G}} - -$$

bo- lo re   pa-   pi-   ha

The antara begins

$$\overset{0}{-} \underset{\smile}{\text{PP}} \underset{\smile}{-\dot{\text{S}} \dot{\text{S}}} \mid \overset{3}{\dot{\text{S}}\text{N}} \dot{\text{R}}\dot{\text{S}} - \mid \overset{+}{\text{P} \text{ N} \dot{\text{S}}\text{N}} \text{ R} \mid \overset{2}{\dot{\text{S}}\text{NDP MP}} \overset{\frown}{\text{m G}}$$

hi-ra mo-ti- yā- na ki   hā- ra di- lā-   ū

FIGURE 5.1   *Khyāl in Rāg Gaur Sārang.*

of a lonely lover who says to the cuckoo, "Take this message to my beloved . . . tell him to bring me necklaces and pearls . . ." We hear the *sarangī* (bowed lute) shadowing the voice, along with a *sarod* and a cello in the background. The tablā plays, *sitārkhāni tāl,* a lilting variation of the sixteen-beat *tintāl.*

WHAT IS A *RĀGA*?

The concept of *rāg* is very elusive. The reason for this is that some *rāg*s are very broad in their possibilities for melodic elasticity and expansion, while others are quite narrow and restrictive: simply stated, there are big *rāg*s and small and everything in between. It is the fixed compositions in any *rāg* which can bring out the most individual features of a *rāg*'s personality, and we again are reminded of the old Sanskrit phrase, *ranjāyati iti rāga:* "that which tinges the mind with color is a *rāga*." Some of the abstract qualities of *rāg* structure are enumerated in Figure 5.2.

1. A *rāga* must have at least five notes, and cannot omit **sa**.
2. Some form of **ma** or **pa** must be present as well.
3. Two forms of the same note adjacent to each other are rarely encountered.
4. A *rāga* uses a certain selection of tones: ones that are omitted are termed "forbidden" and cannot be used without destroying the *rāg*.

FIGURE 5.2   *General qualities common to all* rāgas.

(continued)

5. There is an ascending and descending format.

For *rāg Gaur Sārang* (CD track 24), the ascent may be given as

Ṇ S G R m G P M D P Ṡ N Ṙ Ṡ

and the descent as

Ṡ N D P M P m R G R m G R S

6. Many *rāg*s have strong tonal centers, called *vādi* and *samvādi*. For *Gaur Sārang*, for example, these are **G** and **D** respectively. Typically, these two notes are a fourth or a fifth apart. The *vādi-samvādī* do not substitute for the importance of the tonal center **sa** in a rāg, and do not always function the same way for each *rāg*.

7. Certain moods are typically associated with each *rāg* (see Chapter 2), and often a time of day or season of the year. *Gaur Sārang* is an afternoon *rāg* with the moods of peace and pathos.

8. Prescribed melodic movements that often recur, like catch phrases, identifying the *rāg*. In *Gaur Sārang* one such phrase is **G R m G.**

9. There can be precise use of timbres and tonal shading, heightened by the use of microtonal pitches that vary from one *rāg* to another, lending particular character to the *rāg*. (Considering these variations, one cannot use blanket phrases such as "perfect tuning" or "Indian tuning" to refer to pitch placement.)

FIGURE 5.2 *Continued*

RĀGA IN PERFORMANCE

When a musician performs a *rāg* in *tāl*, he or she bases the performance around a fixed composition (*bandish*), and then adds sections to it. After singing or playing the complete *bandish* a few times, it may be shortened into a refrain, perhaps only the first line of the composition, or even only a few beats leading up to the downbeat of the *tāl*. This foreshortened phrase usually shows a main feature of the *rāg* and is called the *mukhṛā* ("face"). The words *bolo re papīhā* are the *mukhṛā* of the song in *Gaur Sārang* in CD track 24. The *mukhṛā* reappears frequently dur ing a performance, often returning again and again.

The sections that a performer will then add will be determined both by the performance genre and the tradition that the performer represents, as well as the circumstances of the occasion. Because they will be composed on the spot, they will never be reproduced in performance the same way each time. These usually proceed from slow tempos to fast, and are a meditation on the melodic design of the *rāg*. This slow beginning and acceleration to a rapid conclusion is characteristic of Hindustani *rāg* development in general, and is known as the *badhāt* (pronounced "bar-HOT," which means "growth"). The maintenance of the picture, feeling, and design of the slow and steady growth of the *rāg* is a highly prized and satisfying aspect of the performance of mature musicians, one which suggests the growth of a plant from seed to full flowering.

If the prevailing image of the *rāg* in performance were of organic growth and blooming, then the many varieties of flowers would be the *rāg*s themselves. Musicians say that the number of *rāg*s number about 75,000 according to all the mathematical possibilities of note combinations and ordering. In any era, it seems that 500 or so *rāg*s are in circulation, but one musician might know half that many. A good musician may master the performance of only several dozen *rāg*s in his lifetime, although he might recognize many more by their sound. Even then, it is rare for a musician to actually state that he "knows" a *rāg*, since each rendering brings new perspectives. It is told that one master played *rāg Iman Kalyān* on fifty consecutive nights for his royal patron, and each time he brought some new composition, and some new perspective on how this *rāg* might be developed.

THE ON-THE-SPOT DEVELOPMENT OF THE COMPOSITION

The added sections, which comprise the development of the *rāg* in performance, are different in various schools, as well as for instruments and voice. They all share some common factors, although the terminology and techniques may vary quite a bit. The following discussion focuses on the options offered by a performance genre called *khyāl*—the expansive *baṛā* (big) *khyāl*, and the faster *chhotā* (little) *khyāl*.

Baṛā Khyāl. Often, the development of the *rāg* focuses on the syllable. A performer will begin by extending the notes and phrases of the *rāg* in a slow and deliberate manner. These sections are called *vistārs* ("expansions"). In a song, the performer may simply sing "ah," or extend and repeat the vowel sounds of the text. If the text were *e pyārī piyā sanga* ("O, with my dearest beloved . . .") as it is in the performance described next for instance, then the long vowel sounds, ā and ī, would be extended, with the inevitable result that the meaning of the text would be relegated to a minor position.

On CD tracks 25–29, the young vocalist Rashid Khan sings a *baṛā khyāl* in the evening *rāg Bāgeshri*, a *rāga* with flat third and seventh degrees that emphasize the fourth degree (**ma**). Therefore the droning *tānpūra* is tuned to **ma** with the usual **sa**. In this presentation of the *rāg*, the introductory *ālāp* (not heard here) is very short, only a minute or two. The composition (we hear) then begins with the *mukhṛā, pyārī piyā sanga*, which lasts 21 seconds. This *mukhṛā*, in its simplest version (it is later highly ornamented), is shown in Figure 5.3.

$$\overbrace{S^m g^{PS}R}\ S\ \ \overset{\smile}{--D--n--}\ \ \overset{+}{S}\ \ \ S$$

pyā-　　*rī*　*pi- yā*　*san- ga*

FIGURE 5.3　Mukhṛā *in the* Baṛā Khyāl *in* Bāgeshri

But the fixed part of this composition continues on one minute longer until the *mukhṛā* reappears and comes to the downbeat at 1:32. This takes only one cycle of this very slow twelve-beat *tāl* called *ektāl*. The performers are dividing each beat into slow 1/4-beat micropulses of approximately two seconds each, so each "beat" is around six seconds long! The words are used loosely, almost like the vocable syllables of the *dhrupad* compositions, to help with the phrasing.

Vistār.　In the evening *rāg, Bāgeshrī*, the fourth degree of the scale, the note **ma**, is very important. The next section on CD track 26 follows immediately, but we are actually eight minutes later in the composition, and Rashid-ji sings the *vistār* ("expansion") of this important note, **ma**. Shadowed by the reed harmonium he freezes time in landing on and extending this tone. As he brings the world to a halt holding out the note without vibrato, he shows a total concentration on the pitch. There follows a few more *vistārs* of **ma**, and then he returns to a highly ornamented *mukhṛā*, signaling the end of this *vistār*.

Ten minutes later into this performance (CD track 27) he approaches the high **sa** with several vocal flourishes. When he intones **sa**, there is a feeling of climactic arrival: all motion again suddenly stops, and the artist's concentration on intoning the note with the syllable *rī* absorbs his (and our) entire concentration. It is an important point in the exposition of the *rāg*, and a good placement of this final *vistār*—the notes have now all been presented, and the next phase of the *rāg*'s *badhāt* will commence. He returns to the *mukhṛā*.

FIGURE 5.4 Khyāl *artist Rashid Khan sings at the Ali Akbar College. On his lap he strums a swaramandala, a zither that is tuned to the notes of the* rāga. *The large male* tanpura *in the background provides a drone.* *(Photo courtesy of vocalist Tamarind Free Jones.)*

This has been *svār-vistār,* or "note-expansion," where the artist is concentrating on presenting the single tones of the *rāg.* An artist is likely to combine this concentration on the single tones with an elaboration on the context of the note in the *rāg.* He does this with ornaments and combinations of the note with phrases he has previously introduced.

Tān. Further on in his rendition, Rashid further develops the *rāg* with some melodic runs called *tāns* (usually in a faster tempo). These can be of numerous types, including *sārgām tāns* (using the names of the notes), *boltāns* (using the words of the song), or simply *ākār tāns* (using an open-voiced "ah" sound).

In CD track 28, another jump in the performance brings us to the *sārgām tāns*. Heard here is a *tān* (fast passage), taken at a slightly faster tempo, which uses the names of the notes. Rashid-ji shakes each tone slightly with the ornament known as *gamak* (compare it with the *dhrupad gamaks* of CD track 11). A knowledgeable audience will delight in such a display of imagination and virtuosity. He returns to the *mukhṛā* with a great flourish to high **sa**, ending the *tān*.

At the conclusion of both the slow and fast *khyāl* compositions may come the fast runs with "ah" sounds (*ākār tāns*). There are many types of *tāns*, each with a specific melodic or rhythmic quality, described as "jumping," "inverted," "full sweep," "*alankār*" (melodic sequences), "*gamak*," and other similar descriptive terms.

The second movement of a *khyāl* performance, on CD track 29, is in a medium to fast tempo, and is called the *chhotā khyāl* ("small *khyāl*"). These compositions are often in *tintāl* or sometimes in medium *ektāl* (and other *tāls*), and can be subject to the same style of development as the *barā khyāl*—*vistārs* and *tāns*—depending on the training and the mood of the performer. This particular *chhotā khyāl* itself begins with a flourish (*tān*). He sings the first line (the new *mukhṛā*) five times while *tablā* accompanist, Gopal Bandopadhyaya, plays a dazzling short solo.

At the 0:25 mark, Rashid-ji sings the second line of the composition, also fixed. After singing the song through two times, he begins the final section of the performance, with brilliant fast *tāns*, beginning at 0:57, returning to the new *mukhṛā*, *piharama garama lāge*. At 1:19 he sings a *sārgām* tan, and at 1:40 a longer *vistār* of high **sa**, which uses the text of the second section of the song, the *antarā*. He then returns to the first line of the song at 2:15, and later concludes the performance with several minutes of fast *tāns* (not heard here).

Khyāl *and Instrumental Styles.* The shape and mood of the *chhota khyāl* have influenced instrumental music to varying degrees, and CD track 30 presents a *khyāl* composed and played by the famous *sitarist*, Vilayat Khan, who calls his style *gāyakī ang*, "singing style." This excerpt from a private house concert begins with the Vilayat Khan singing (along with a second unknown vocalist) the *chhotā khyāl, sakhi*

Rashid Khan sings *Rag Bāgeshri*

CD track 25	*Mukhrā* beginning *barā khyāl*
0:13	Downbeat (*sam*) of slow *ektāl*, entry of *tablā*
0:21	End of *mukhrā*
1:32	Second cycle downbeat, end of fixed composition
CD track 26	Jump ahead in performance to beginning of *ma vistār*
0:54	*Mukhrā* (ornamented) ending this vistar of *ma*
CD track 27	Jump ahead in performance to high *sa vistār*
1:04	*Mukhrā* ending *sa vistār*
CD track 28	Jump ahead to *sārgām tān*
0:46	*Mukhrā* ending *sārgām tān*
CD track 29	Jump ahead to beginning of *chhotā khyāl* in medium *tintāl*
0:25	Second line of *chhotā khyāl*
0:51	End of fixed composition (*bandish* of *chhotā khyāl*)
0:57	Beginning of *tāns* (*ākār*, "ah" *tān*)
1:19	*Sārgām tān*
1:23	*Chhotā khyāl bandish* (both lines)
1:40	*Antarā* in *vistār* style (high *sa*)

FIGURE 5.5 *Listening Guide:* Rāg Bāgeshri.

mori rhuma jhuma ghara āyi ("my beloved enters swinging and swaying") in medium *tintāl*. They sing the two-lined composition, and then Khansahib plays the *sitār*, accompanied by *tablist* Zakir Hussain, whose lilting accompaniment gives this performance rare life. At 1:06, the second section of the composition, the *antarā*, begins with the words *āyi nāchi* ("she came dancing . . ."). It includes part of a famous dance composition (*kita taka tun tun na*), and ends with a *sārgām tān*.

SONG TEXTS IN CLASSICAL STYLES

The texts of many *dhrupads*, *khyāls*, and *bhajans* were composed by the poets of the Bhakti Movement, a devotional tide that swept over North India from the south in the fifteenth century and enjoyed a great flowering for the next two hundred years (see Chapter 2). Sharing some ideals with the Protestant Reformation in Europe, the Bhakti Movement favored vernacular languages and an individual's relationship to God as being more important than the formal language (Sanskrit) or the strict regulations of organized religion. Later, in the late seventeenth century, another style of poetry became popular, the *rīti*, or mannerist, school. This often used stock images and settings (hence "mannerist") celebrating female beauty, unrequited love, and domestic life in the large collective families. Love songs abound in this style, in which the lover is often alone, waiting for the arrival of the lover who is away. The text of *rāg Gaur Sārang* (CD track 24) is of this type, as is the *rhuma jhuma* song of Vilayat Khan (CD track 30).

An important parallel of the otherwise predominantly Hindu Bhakti Movement was the rise in popularity of the Islamic Sufi sects in India. Sufism is a mystic branch of Islam, but individual schools of the Sufi orders follow the teachings of particular teachers, who, while embracing traditional Islam, emphasize a personalized approach, devotional immediacy, and toleration for many styles of worship. Their fervent devotional emphasis on love placed the Sufis in alignment with the Hindu's expression of *bhakti* (devotion). Moreover, since many Hindu musicians needed to convert to Islam in order to secure positions at the Muslim courts (where they often took the name "Khan"), the latitude, openness, and kinship of the Sufis with the Hindu Bhaktis made the changeover more attractive. A favorite type of song of the Sufis is the *qawwālī*, which enjoyed a great surge in international popularity in the late twentieth century and continuues today with singing of the Sabri Brothers and late Nusrat Fateh Ali Khan.

OTHER SONG GENRES

The film song (*filmi gīt*, refer to CD track 1) and the *ghazal* are the most popular song genres of North India. Along with the *bhajan* (CD track 13), the *ghazal* (CD track 31) has greatly influenced the film song. Coming to full flower in classical literature in Delhi in the eighteenth century, the *ghazal* is an Urdu-language poetic form fashioned in rhymed couplets, usually telling a story of unrequited love and longing. Ambiguity in the classical *ghazal* usually revolves around addressing the beloved: is it a woman or a metaphor for God? The images are often stock: the night, the stars, intoxication, wine, a tavern as a temple, among others. The film *ghazal* and its modern pop-song derivatives use some of these images, but most of the time the beloved is a woman or man. Many *ghazal*s are clearly devotional, many are simply love songs, and many are both.

The Gramophone Company of India (now a subsidiary of EMI) began recording light-classical music in India in the first years of the twentieth century, and by 1910 there were more than 4000 titles in circulation. A genre that received much attention during this time was the *ghazal*.

Ghazal, Fana kais bana kaisī, ghazal in Rāg Bhairavi
sung by Jankibai, CD track 42
translated by Peter Manuel

0:00	A	*What are life and death when one is aware of Him?*
0:13	A	Repeat
0:22	A	*We enter into that house and descend to this house.*
0:31	B	*What is the relationship between Mohammad and Joseph?*
0:40	B'	Repeat
0:52	C	*Joseph was a suitor of Zuleikha while Mohammad was beloved of God*
1:00	A	Repeat
1:09	D	*Christ dwells in the seventh heaven*
1:17	D	Repeat
1:26	E	*But the Prophet is in the highest heaven.*
1:33	E	Repeat
1:44	D	*When I have surrendered, then it is only me alone*
1:52	D	Repeat
1:59	B	*At times I am created, at times I am my own god.*

FIGURE 5.6   *Listening Guide.*

The early *ghazal* recordings featured mostly women from a class of entertainers called *baijis,* who have some parallel with the geishas of Japan.

> *These highly accomplished ladies were great favorites of the royalty, landlords, and merchants; some even had amorous liaisons with them. They were extremely knowledgeable in music, dance, literature, shairi (the recitation of Urdu and Persian couplets), and many other arts, blessed with good looks and attractive personalities, beautiful manners and speech, and also an advanced sexual knowledge of the Kāma Sutra. The rich and the aristocracy would send their adoles-*

cent sons to these courtesans in order to receive an all-round
education!

Ravi Shankar, Ragamala

As an artistic community, they now retain only a shadow of their former glory, for they were the bearers not only of a rich music and dance legacy, but also of a learned and refined culture that functioned as an arm of court life. Ladies of this society had *-bai* added as a suffix to their name, such as Jankibai, who sings the *ghazal* on CD track 31. On this very early recording—1908—Jankibai sings a *ghazal* in the *rāg Bhairavi.* The rhythm is one of the many varieties of eight-beat *tāls* called *kaharwā.* The text is devotional, and is derived from stories in the *Koran.* Often the lines of each couplet are repeated. There are only four fundamental lines of melody (A, B, C, and D below, with B nearly the same as E), but each is repeated with a great deal of ornamentation, so a casual listening might neither reveal the simplicity of the song nor the intricate artistry of Jankibai.

CONCLUSION

From the Vedic chant to Lata Mangeshkar to Jagjit Singh (see CD track 42), India is steeped in song of every variety. In the lighter genres, the idea of *rāg* and its various types of regulated, stylized, and improvisatory performance formats are usually left behind—although there is a lingering suggestion of the melodic color of *rāg* in occasional songs. In the classical styles, the song is used as a springboard for the development of the *rāga*, and the artists ability to compose *vistār*s and *tān*s on the spot becomes the main concentration of the performance (often leaving the song and its meaning far behind). The range of texts runs the gamut from the verbal syllable to devotional poetry, from linguistically-meaningless rhythmic sounds to very explicit images from classical and modern poetic sources. The great range of styles and genres makes Indian song a feast for the ear, and one that attracts and involves musicians on many levels, from devotional singers to virtuoso concert artists to popular superstars. One thing is sure, to be involved in Indian music on any level, is to sing; and further, to be absorbed in a gamut of explorational possibilities between fixed composition and improvisation.

The next chapter explores some of the same ideas from the perspective of instrumental music.

CHAPTER 6

Instruments, Melodic and Rhythmic

There is a saying in India, "Every ten miles you walk brings a new dialect." If this hints at the truth, then it should come as no surprise that there are endless varieties in all the arts and crafts—another facet of the encounter with the concept of fixed versus improvised. In Europe, musical instruments were standardized so that they could be used interchangeably in ensembles such as orchestras, bands, string quartets, and brass choirs. In India, by contrast, a predilection for solo timbres has resulted in many individual styles and innovations in instrument construction. To cite an instance, there are several different kinds of *sitār*s. Vilayat Khan's *sitār* is different from Ravi Shankar's, and Nikhil Banerjee's sounds very different from either of them. In addition, instruments from different regions may share the same name, but be quite different in construction. Now at the dawn of the twenty-first century, the idea of "standard" instruments is starting to enter into the manufacturing of Indian instruments, but there is still a great scope in sizes, shapes, and sounds among instruments having the same name. You may reread the account of my visit to the instrument maker's shop in Chapter 1 for an idea of how this variety is managed.

Throughout history, there has been much exchange of Indian musical instruments with those of other cultures, and this vigorous international trade shows no sign of letting up. India has borrowed as many instruments as she has given, and continues to modify both her own as well as the ones she borrows. A tenth-century temple frieze from South India shows a person playing a bowed instrument supported at his neck—could it be a prototypical violin? Today the violin is played all over India, in classical concerts and film scores, but this modern instrument was reimported from Europe in the eighteenth century.

Lutes, zithers, and dulcimers (a kind of zither) abound in ancient organology, and these have traveled throughout the world. The *santūr* is a hammered dulcimer found in India and West Asia; it traveled east along the storied Silk Road ending up in China as the *yangqin*, and in the West eventually as the piano. Many ancient Indian sculptures show plucked lutes, which seem like ancestors of the *sarod*, but the modern form of this instrument shares strong West Asian roots. Thus hundreds of instruments have come and gone, and as artists who played them have altered their preferences, they have modified and combined the old instruments to become the new. In India today, guitars, cellos, and saxophones take their place alongside traditional *vīnas*, *sarangīs*, and bamboo flutes in contemporary musical life, as composers seek the sound of music that will keep their work before the public.

Classifying instruments is an ancient practice. In the *Natyasāstra*, the famous treatise on music, dance, and drama from around the fourth century CE, instruments are described as belonging in four categories. (In 1914, some fifteen centuries later, these categories became the basis for the Sachs-Hornböstel system of instrument classification that is now widely used.) The instruments were categorized according to their primary means of producing sound. Strings (chordophones) were called *tata*; lutes, zithers, harps and lyres are subcategories of chordophones. Winds (aerophones) were called *suṣhīra*; drums (membranophones) were *avanaddha*; and percussion instruments (non-drums, metallophones, or idiophones) were *ghana*. Recently, instruments that used electronic means of sound generation (a fifth category: electrophones) have been added to the system, but instruments in the first four categories have abundant examples in India. Another way to classify instruments is by their function, discussed here by whether they are used to play the background drone, and the lead or accompanying melody.

DRONE INSTRUMENTS

One instrument that is usually a part of every ensemble is the long-necked lute-zither, the *tānpurā* (sometimes spelled *tamboura*), which is a stringed drone instrument (Figure 6.1). It is not entirely clear how long Hindustani music has been thought of as having a fixed tonal center, and eventually incorporating a drone background played by an instrument designated for that purpose. Some trace the practice back to the droning of the *Rig Veda* (CD track 4); others theorize that it came into practice with the lutes of the ninth century CE. It began to take its place as a regular member of a classical ensemble at the beginning of the seventeenth century, as musicians in the Mughul court adapted a West

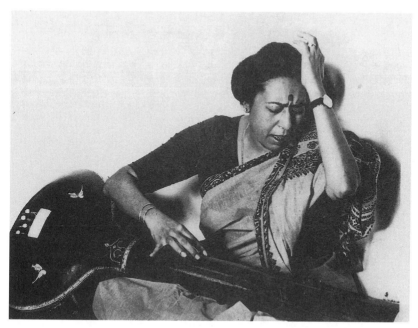

FIGURE 6.1 Khyāl *singer Prabha Atre in concert. She plays the* tānpurā *across her lap, and raises her hand in a flourish which coincides with the passionate movement of the singing.* Khyāl *singers are often known for their animated gestures while they sing.*

Asian lute (*tambur*) for this new purpose. Frets on that instrument were eliminated. The buzzing timbre (*javarī*) that is produced by the strings vibrating across a flat-topped bridge is characteristic of the sound of the *tānpurā*, and could hardly have developed without the advent of steel strings in the seventeenth century.

The sound of a droning *tānpurā* serves two important functions: one, it frames the music, giving the musician a background of uniform sound upon which to sing or play, and creates an ambient quietness, like incense, which fills the atmosphere with mood. Second, it intones the tonal center, the **sa** (usually along with the fifth or fourth), maintaining a pitch reference, and helping the musician stay in tune. *Tānpurā*s come in all sizes; the larger ones used for vocal accompaniment have sound chambers made out of large dried gourds, and the smaller ones, used for instrumental accompaniment are often flatter and made entirely of wood.

FIGURE 6.2 *Laxmi Shankar sings* khyāl *in concert. She strums a* swaramandala *as she pauses to exchange glances with the* tablā *player. Vocalist Julie Ann Johnson plays the* tānpurā.

The *tānpurā*'s long, unfretted neck is hollow—which technically places it in the class of zithers, although the long neck relates it to the lute family.

Other instruments are used as drones, as well, such as small pumped reed boxes (*surpeti*), and nowadays one often hears an electronic version of a *tānpurā* or *surpeti* quietly droning in the background. These small "drone machines" are easier to transport than a *tānpurā*, and they do not require an extra performer. Again, these drones—zithers, lutes, reeds, as well as harps—may have ancient roots as reinforcements of the focal pitch **sa**, the intoning of which can be heard as far back as in the chanting of the Vedas (CD track 4).

MELODY INSTRUMENTS

Melodically, an instrumental soloist needs to be able to do three things in order to play in the traditional classical styles: she or he should be able to slide between notes, rendering certain instruments with fixed-pitch placement less desirable. The player also needs to be able to microtonally alter some of the pitches to accommodate the subtleties of tuning that are required in different *rāg*s. And the soloist must be able to play the quick and subtle ornaments—turns, mordents, and *gamaks*—that are not easy to play on instruments with keys or frets. Ideally, then, the instrumentalist should be able to slide between the notes, play minute pitch variations, and execute quick ornaments without being bound by a tempered tuning system, or the keys, valves, and frets which are so necessary for precise ensemble playing. But, since modern styles in India often encompass Western models, so too, have many Western-style instruments found a home, especially in the film and recording studios.

The Rise of Instrumental Music. In the minds of earlier generations, the voice was the primary vehicle of classical music. If an instrument were used to accompany the voice, it was deemed a secondary instrument and the player hence lost the social prestige of a soloist. A famous legend concerning the famous eighteenth century *rudra vīna* player, Niyāmat Khan, tells that he fled his post at the court of the emperor rather than be ordered to serve as an accompanist. He must have been a great player: the emperor is said to have requested his return and acceded to his wishes to only be a soloist—an unprecedented personal assertion for a musician of his era. This legend, whether true or not, signaled the beginning of the rise of instrumental music in the modern eras.

Since Mughal times (the sixteenth through the nineteenth centuries), chordophones have been the primary instruments of classical music. In ancient times, *vīnas* in great variety were described; however, most of these were harps and lyres. The *rudra vīna* is a stick-zither, which dominated the Mughul period and persisted through the twentieth century. Now called the *bīn*, the *rudra vīna* is fading fast from modern performances. It became so highly treasured, and players of it so specialized, that teachers became protective of its technique and learning, and would teach it only to family members.

THE *SITĀR* AND THE *SAROD*

In the eighteenth century, the *sitār* developed from a mixing of the Persian *tānpur* and the *rudra vīna*. Eventually its players proved that it

FIGURE 6.3   *Ravi Shankar*, sitār, *with Ali Akbar Khan*, sarod.

was more versatile, louder, and capable of the faster tempos of modern music, so it has gradually replaced the older *bīn*. For many, the
sitār symbolizes the music of North India (Figure 6.3). The image of
Ravi Shankar teaching Beatle George Harrison is iconographic: one of
the great masters of "the East" reaching to "the West" through a young
pop idol of the 1960s. The instrument had become central to the musical image of North India by the late nineteenth century. As young British
women of breeding might have been expected to have parlor skills on
the piano, so the *sitār* became the rising middle-class image of culture
and cultivation. While it still holds some of that position, it is not an
easy instrument to play, and frustrates anyone without a serious dedication to master it.

The same difficulty might be attributed to its sister instrument, the
sarod (Figure 6.3), although it has never enjoyed the vogue of the *sitār*.
But both instruments are at the top of the pedestal of Hindustani classical music, for they have inherited the technique and literature of the
rudra vīna as well as having their own distinctive voices. The *sarod*
and *sitār* have similarities in timbre, but their playing techniques are

quite different. The most striking difference is that on a *sitār* the slides between the notes are effected by pulling the playing string across the curved frets on the neck, whereas the *sarod* player uses his fingernail on a fretless steel fingerboard to obtain a similar sound.

The rigor of the training of a classical instrumentalist is described by Ravi Shankar as he took a lesson from his new guru, Allauddin Khan:

> Once, when I had first come to him and he was teaching me an exercise, I was not able to play it correctly. "Ha!" he exclaimed, "You have no strength in those wrists. Da, da, da," he cried, as he smacked my hands. Well, I had been trying my best, and I felt terrible that he should be angry with me. From my childhood, no one had ever spoken angrily to me, although I was quite spoiled and sometimes behaved badly. So when Baba raised his voice to me, I began to get angry myself, rather than frightened. "Go," he taunted me, "go, go and buy some bangles to wear on your wrists. You are like a weak little girl! You have no strength. You can't even do this exercise."
>
> That was enough for me. I got up and went to the house next door where I had been staying, packed my bedding and belongings, marched off to the railroad station, and bought a ticket home. I had just missed a train and had to wait a while for the next one. In the meantime, Ali Akbar came running up and, seeing my bags, asked what happened. "I won't stay," I told him. "He scolded me today."
>
> Ali Akbar looked at me incredulously and asked if I were mad. "You are the *only* person he has never laid a hand on. We're all amazed by it. Why, do you know what he has done to me? He's tied me to a tree every day for a week and beaten me and even refused me food. And you run away because he gives you a little scolding!" Adamantly I insisted, "No, I will leave on the evening train."
>
> Ali Akbar persuaded me to go back to the house with him, and I temporarily set my bag down again in my room. By then, he had told his mother what happened, and she told Baba. Ali Akbar came to tell me they wanted me to have lunch with them, and when I went into the house, Ma (Ali Akbar's mother) said to me, "Come. You are leaving soon, but just go and sit with your Baba for a few minutes." I went over to him and did a *pranām* [respectful gesture to a *guru*], and I saw that he was cutting out a photograph of me and putting it into a frame. Neither of us said a word, but I saw that he was moved. After a little while, I finally said, "I am going today." Slowly, he looked over at me, and asked,

"Is that all? I mean, I just told you to wear bangle bracelets and it has hurt you so much that you are going to leave?" I had tears in my eyes already, and had never seen him like this. He stood up and came over to me, and said, "You remember at the pier in Bombay how your mother put your hand in mine and asked me to look after you as my own son? Since then, I have accepted you as my son, and this is how you want to break it?" Naturally, I didn't leave Baba after this scene. (*My Music, My Life*, 72-3)

For many, *sitārist* Ravi Shankar and sarodist Ali Akbar Khan (Figure 6.3) have provided a high-water mark in modern Hindustani instrumental music. Trained together by the legendary Allauddin Khan, Ali Akbar's father and one of the great musical figures of the early part of the twentieth century, these two have brought their exciting styles and high virtuosity into every corner of the earth, especially in their hundreds of concerts in Europe and America. We will now examine some music in the styles Allauddin Khan's students.

The Sitār *and the* Sarod.   This section introduces instrumental style through a famous *sarod* recording of one of its preeminent masters, Ali Akbar Khan. CD track 32 (See Figure 6.5 for a timed listening guide) is an example of the evening rāga *Chandranandan,* Ali Akbar Khan plays a quick introduction on his *sarod* and then, at the 0:27 mark, plays the descending *mukhrā* leading to the downbeat of *tintāl*. He plays an ornamented version of the *gat* (fixed composition) for three cycles of the *tāl*. *Tablist* Mahapurush Misra plays a short introductory solo, which lasts one cycle and emphasizes the downbeat in closing.

$$\text{nd} \left| \overset{3}{\text{P nd}} \ \overline{\text{dP}}\text{m} \ \text{d-Pm} \right| \overset{+}{\text{G}}$$

FIGURE 6.4   Mukhrā *in* rāg Chandranandan

At 1:04 there is a *vistār* (improvised developmental section) played on the *sarod* that lasts two cycles until the *mukhrā* returns at 1:24. The *tablā* player plays a variation that also lasts two cycles. *Now you have grasped the basic format of the instrumental gat presentation format*—the alternation of solos by instrumentalist and drummer. The instrumentalist signals his return by playing the *mukhrā*, the *tablā* player returns with a *tihāī* (although these signals have many variations). The melodic artist builds the *vistār*s by increasing the range and rhythmic variety until he reaches and explores the upper register of the *rāg*.

In CD track 33 (considerably further along in the same performance), Ali Akbar begins to work intensively with the rhythm, playing with off

Ali Akbar Khan, *sarod,* plays *Rāg Chandranandan*

CD track 32	After two strums of the open strings on his instrument, he plays a several phrases from the *rāg* as an introduction; this short style is known as *aochar ālāp*
0:27	*Mukhrā* to the fixed composition (*gat*) in slow *tintāl Tablā* enters with a short solo
0:41	*Mukhrā* to *gat* returns, a variation of *gat*
0:55	*Mukhrā*
1:04	*Vistār,* lower-mid register, ends with medium-speed *tān*
1:24	*Mukhrā* returns, *tablā* solo (two cycles)
1:56	Low register *vistār,* gradually ascends to middle **ga**
2:48	*Mukhra* to *tablā* solo beginning with triplets, ending in fast duple rhythm
3:17	*Vistār* in middle register
3:47	*Tān* in style with mainly down-strokes of right hand with *tihāī* at 3:52, continues with *vistārs* to *antarā* (high register)
4:55	*Tān* ends with *mukhrā* at 5:21
CD track 33	Jump ahead in performance to section of rhythmic variation, first with off-beats; then mixed with right-hand stroke patterns, consciously maintaining the off-beat inflection
1:18	*Tihāī,* then *mukhrā,* ends this off-beat *tān*
CD track 34	Jump ahead in performance to fast *gat* in *tintāl*
0:13	Second line of composition ending in *tān*-like flourish
0:26	Variations of first line of *gat*
0:47	*Tān* with down-strokes
0:57	*Tān* continues in larant style, using the repeated **sa** as a springboard for neighbor-note motion around it
CD track 35	Beginning of *jhālā* section with repeated rhythmic striking of the high drone strings
CD track 36	Beginning of *sawāl-jawāb* (question-answer) section with *tablā*
1:56	Tightening (like a concluding stretto) of the responses begins
2:39	Fast *jhālā*
2:55	Fast *tān* finishing in *chakradār tihāī* on high **sa**

FIGURE 6.5 *Listening guide: Ali Akbar Khan.*

beats and syncopations deliberately composed to sound counter to the regularity of the *tablā* beat. This is what is called *layakari*, "playing with the rhythm," a manifestation of this artist's deep grounding in the *dhrupad* tradition, where rhythmic design is given this kind of rigor (refer back to CD track 11).

In CD track 34, the fast composition (*gat*) is presented with its regular rhythmic pattern (123,123 . . .) articulated by the *sarodist*'s right hand plucking patterns. These patterns are probably even more ancient, but were written down 800 years ago. The artist puts these rhythms through a series of quick variations until settling into a traditionally structured *tān* at the 0:47 mark.

In CD track 35 Ali Akbar eases into the final section, the *jhālā* ("sparkling"), characterized by repeated quick strokes of the drone strings. Playing with energy and elan, the artists arrive at the final section, the "question-answer" (*sawāl-jawāb*) exchange, in CD track 36. This part is very popular with live audiences, where the melodic soloist plays a rhythm and the *tablā* player answers with an imitation, or a variation based on the same idea. The exchanges finally telescope (become shorter and quicker) until the performance ends with a thrilling *tihāī* played together.

The late Nikhil Banerjee (1931–1986) had a unique playing style that was also greatly shaped by his studies with Allauddin Khan. In this example of a *gat* in the rare *rāg Sindhūr-Khammāj*, Nikhil-ji (Figure 6.6) plays a highly structured *gat* in a traditional style (contrast this with Vilayat Khan in CD track 30). Despite his use of *rubato* (playing with the regularity of the rhythm), the artist plays in the very classical *gat-torā* style (a theme-and-variations format) developed in the eighteenth century and further refined in the nineteenth century. While it might be true that all *gat*s are compositions articulated with plucking patterns (*bols*), this particular style is defined by the use of certain characteristic plucking patterns of the right hand in both the fixed composition (the *gat* proper) and the variations (*torā*).

At the 0:37 mark in CD track 37 he plays the *antarā* or contrasting higher section, again quite traditionally structured by the plucking patterns. This part ends with a flourishing *tān* and returns to the *gat* proper. At the 1:13 point, he begins the sitar *jhālā*, which "sparkles" indeed with repeated strokes of the drone strings of his *sitār*.

OTHER MELODY INSTRUMENTS

Whereas the *sitār* and *sarod* have held a preeminent position in the instrumental tradition by virtue of their versatility and inheritance of the

FIGURE 6.6 *The late* sitārist *Nikhil Banerjee in a classroom demonstration. Notice that the* sitār's *main string runs down the middle of the fingerboard, not along the edge like most lutes and guitars. The movable frets are curved, which allow for the characteristic slides and ornaments, and this takes great strength and much practice.*

dhrupad instrumental techniques of the older *vina*s and *rabāb*s (a plucked lute found also in the West Asian tradition), other players have brought different instruments to the classical stage in the latter part of the twentieth century. The *santūr* is a hammered dulcimer of a type found in the West and all along the Silk Road into China. In India, Kashmir is its home, but it is now played throughout the North. Initially, it would seem unlikely that such an instrument would be accepted as classical, since a hammered dulcimer, with its fixed-string arrangement, is incapable of slides and certain types of ornaments. Indeed, older players scoffed when it was first presented on the classical stage. But what it has lacked in these dimensions its players have made up for by using variation in dynamics, speed, and rhythmic excitement, which, by the end of the twentieth century, has given Indian *santūr* players a large following around the world.

CD track 38 begins with a *tān* that shows the range of the *santūr*, from low to high, in the hands of Shivkumar Sharma. The instrument is played with two small hammers, and their bouncing produces a clicking sound. Zakir Hussain plays the *tablā* in fast *tintāl*. The rhythmic structure of Shivkumar-ji's *bandish* (fixed composition) is 7 + 7 + 5, and Zakir-ji answers with a *tablā* solo which is made up of this rhythm derived from the composition, finishing with a dramatic *tihāī* which comes to beat 14—the beginning point of the theme in the rhythmic cycle. The audience appreciates this display of mathematics and exciting virtuosity.

$$D - n \left| \overset{+}{-} \overset{\cdot}{S} \, n \, D' \right| \overset{2}{G} - m - \left| \overset{0}{D} \, m \, G' \, \underset{\cdot}{n} \right| \overset{3}{S} \, \underset{\cdot}{D} - \underset{\cdot}{n} \left| \overset{+}{S} \right.$$

FIGURE 6.7   *Theme from* santūr *solo of Shivkumar Sharma.*

Other instruments and their players have not been so fortunate. The *sarangī the* small bowed lute, has mostly been an instrument of accompaniment (Figure 6.8). As a result it has been thought of as an instrument of a lower class of musician—high irony for one of the most soulful and versatile imitators of the human voice—and now struggles for its very existence. This beautiful instrument has three playing strings and more than thirty-five sympathetic strings, and is played by touching the gut strings on the side (rather than pressing them down), which allows the player very liquid motion in his slides.

Sarangī master Sultan Khan, CD track 39, first sings a folk song from Rajasthan, the picturesque desert region of western India. It is in the folk *tāl* of *dādra*, six beats. He then plays the same melody on his *sarangī*, and the echoey sound of the sympathetic strings gives the melody a haunting timbre.

Several newcomers to the classical world have come from the folk music realm. The image and reality of the old classical masters restricting the music to only include blood members of the family has been thoroughly dashed by several factors over the recent decades, in-

FIGURE 6.8 *Druba Ghosh plays* sarangī. *The* sarangī *(from* sau = *one hundred and* rang = *color) has a very evocative, sometimes wailing, sound, which can be hauntingly similar to the human voice. The strings are not pressed down on the fingerboard like a violin or cello, but rather pressed against the side with the cuticle of the fingernail, so that slides can be effectively played. Note the many resonant sympathetic strings.*

cluding virtuoso performers who have come onto the stage and demanded the attention of the audience through their mastery of their craft. Instruments heretofore thought of as suitable only for folk airs now play the *rāg*s and *tāl*s of the classical tradition with subtlety and virtuosity. These include the double-reed *shāhnāi* and the transverse

FIGURE 6.9 *G. S. Sachdev is a well-known* bānsurī *(bans = bamboo, and* sūr = *note) player. Note that his long flute has no modal points (where branches grew), which gives it a very pure sound. There are no keys like western flutes. The middle parts of his fingers cover the holes, which allows him to roll his fingers over the holes to create the slides and subtleties of pitch necessary in the playing of classical music.*

flute, the *bānsurī* (Figure 6.9), which are both keyless aerophones whose holes are stopped directly with the fingers. The players must master difficult whole- and half-hole fingerings to execute the microtones and slides. It is only in the last sixty years or so that instrumentalists have shown that these instruments are capable of the range of expression heretofore thought of only as in the realm of the classical players.

To many, Hariprasad Chaurasia's flute (CD track 40) is the quintessential sound of India, because he has played folk and popular melodies on so many recordings and for films. More recently, he has become an international figure on the concert stage. In this excerpt, he plays a *peshkār*, a "presentation"—a new theme with a new rhythm—within the larger presentation of the classical *rāg Jāyatshrī*. He begins by playing the scale of the *rāg* up and down. Note the pentatonic scale with a lowered second degree. The example highlights the *peshkār*, which is characterized by staccato tones in a seven-beat rhythm to which he appends *tāns*—quick runs and a series of variations, all of which return to the theme. Fazal Qureshi, son of Alla Rakha accompanies in the seven-beat *tāl* known as *rupak*.

The brass reed was invented in 1815 in Vienna, and by the 1840s had been incorporated into a reed organ called the harmonium, a parlor instrument that played and sustained the notes by being pumped with a pedal bellows somewhat like an organ. Christian missionaries brought harmoniums with them to India to accompany hymn singing. Before long, it was made into a small wooden instrument with the bellows pumped with one hand while the player, seated cross-legged on the floor, played the keyboard with the other. It was ideal for leading the group singing of hymns and *bhajan*s, because it was loud enough to keep a group of singers on pitch. It was decried in classical circles because of its tempered tuning which was deemed detrimental to the music. As time went on, though, it became more and more accepted as a classical instrument to accompany voice, and one occasionally even hears a harmonium solo. The harmonium is heard accompanying both vocalists Rashid Khan (CD track 25) and Anup Jalota (CD track 13).

The guitar has become an important instrument in solo recitals. It is played lying across the lap of the player, "Hawaiian style," with a steel slide held in the left hand and with fingerpicks on the right.

ENSEMBLES

In the film and pop studios of the larger cities, one hears all the instruments, especially the Western ones, played in styles ranging from Indian classical to world-beat. It is not unusual to hear a saxophone, trumpet, piano, banjo, electric guitar, or mandolin in this type of mix, which can sound both Western and distinctly Indian according to the arranger and the players, as well as the use of harmony, heterophony, and solo timbres.

But ensemble music is not new to India. Ancient treatises imply that music was played in ensembles when accompanying dramatic productions. Relief sculptures on temple walls often show groups of instrumentalists, presumably playing together. The ensembles were comprised of various combinations of a half dozen string and wind instruments with percussion, and were used in ceremonies, processions, and in dramatic performances. In the medieval period, the Mughal emperors had their impressive *naubat* ensembles of nine to twenty players including double-reed *sūrnais* (*shahnāis*), horns, trumpets, kettle-drum, cymbals, and other percussion. Contemporary accounts report that this band played regularly when the emperor was in residence, and that it was capable of both sublime majesty and delicate mood.

Allauddin Khan, Timir Baran, Ali Akbar Khan, Ravi Shankar, and a number of other classical instrumentalists have made orchestral arrangements of traditional music. And of course, ensemble music playing in the background of solo voices is the norm in dance productions and most filmscoring, which often uses Western and even electronic instruments to achieve dramatic affects and moods. And street bands abound—from military brass bands, to percussion groups, to wedding bands that feature a wailing clarinet backed by trumpets and drums.

CONCLUSION

For the last one hundred years, instrumental music has steadily increased in quantity, variety, and popularity. And, because the music has moved beyond its courtly environment, musicians have emerged and been acclaimed who have played instruments traditionally thought to have been the province of folk and other cultures. Perhaps because instrumentalists do not use Indian languages that are foreign to many international ears, instrumentalists have gained wide acceptance outside India. Virtuosos have toured the world bringing great renown to their musical tradition.

CHAPTER 7

The Old World Joins the New

THE POSTCOLONIAL ERA

At the end of the twentieth century, India's classical music found itself, in at least one sense, in a cultural parallel with Europe at the end of the eighteenth century. Imagine the world of Mozart and Beethoven, as they created newness within an older language to give their music lustrous vitality in the face of momentous social changes. In the case of Mozart, he never found the secure patronage either with the church or with the nobility, both of which institutions had supported musicians for centuries. In the case of Beethoven, he was his own person—yet still he depended on the support of the aristocracy. His music speaks of a heroic and triumphant emergence of a new social optimism which came out of the turmoil of the revolutions in France and America. In India, the personality profiles may be different, but the social changes that affect the music have striking similarities.

Before the coming of the Europeans, Western scholars and tradesmen raved about India, much as the world raves about America today as the land of opportunity. By the end of the eighteenth century, the British had driven out all other mercantile and political competitors, and declared the Raj in 1858—it was the virtual annexation of India. But colonization has left India a poor country, and from a land rich in both natural resources, production, and centers of higher learning, it has became a debtor nation with great burdens of overpopulation, poverty, and illiteracy.

In throwing off the chains of colonial control by the British in 1947, India did not fall back to her ancient feudal system, with its princes, palaces, *rāja*s and *nawāb*s; rather, she opted for a new democratic system of government—a radical departure from her past. The process of adjusting to the new system has often been challenged by the regional disparities of language, religious sectarianism, and local traditions. The federal government has had to supervise the development of a viable economic system that seeks to accommodate huge contrasts in wealth, literacy, and cultural variety. With one eye toward increasing industrial production and world trade, India has also had to focus on the pressing problems of educating and feeding her population of over one billion people.

THE EFFECT OF THE NEW DEMOCRACY ON MUSIC

It should come as no surprise that artists have also had to make many changes in order to come to grips with the new social realities. Fifty-plus years after independence, it is still a new world: and while some "stars" have done well, it is quite difficult, even with good training, for most artists to make a living in the modern musical environment. The musician must inure himself to travelling frequently and packaging his musical product for an audience not always sure of what it is seeking. The older artists sigh: "They are watering-down the music, trying to make it easy for simple-minded and fickle audiences who are chasing one star today, and a new one tomorrow. The idea of purity in the old music is fading."

However, modern audiences might find the older concert style slow moving and tedious. They want more variety in the mood, melody, and rhythm—and speed.

All the young tablā players are so concerned with speed. They just want to play railās [the compositions with many fast repeated figures]. Nowadays, I am concentrating on teaching the old compositions—from one hundred years ago. I know that it will take the students a lot of time and patience to work on them. But at least this old style will not die, it will not vanish. In those days, the people did not play that fast, like the players are doing today. Every composition, everything has a limit, and if you cross that limit, it is like asking an eighty-year-old man, "C'mon, run!"

The compositions have their set rhythm and tempo, and if you follow that, you will get that whole music. This modern way of playing, well, it is like noise, it is entertaining for the audience, but it is giving you only a shock—"wow!"— but it's not staying. It is useless. From my judgement, in the older time they were simpler—they were looking for the beauty—and we are not doing that. The young players, they are into making fun out of it. But it's not. You cannot make fun out of music. You have to surrender yourself, you have to learn, you have to pay the proper respect. Then you get the music. Otherwise, you're playing only the beat—noise to please the audience—you are not playing music. If you get that music, then there is something new, something beautiful, every time. Balance, clarity, mood . . . right into your heart.

Swapan Chaudhuri

FIGURE 7.1   *Allauddin Khan and Kanthe Maharaj, two immortal players from the early part of the twentieth century. Allauddin Khan, a left-handed* sarod *player, raises his hand at a climactic point in the recital. The great* tablā *player from Benares, Kanthe Maharaj, registers his delighted astonishment. Allauddin Khan, teacher of Ravi Shankar and Ali Akbar Khan, was one of the great innovators. Drinking deeply of all the classical instrumental and vocal styles, he fashioned a new approach to instrumental music.*

The *tablā* is an instrument that has helped construct many bridges across styles and cultures. In North India, it has become the percussion instrument of preference, from classical music to pop. Even in the West, it is now common to hear the *tablā* on pop and jazz recordings as well as in television commercials and movie soundtracks. A number of innovative ensembles use the *tablā* in combination with other drums and instruments.

Sample This (CD track 41) is the beginning of a recording by the Toronto Tablā Ensemble, a group of *tablā* players under the leadership of Ritesh Das, who, with other musicians, play western trap-drum set, bass, *tānpurā*, marimbas and other instruments. Here they create ostinato patterns—influenced by African rhythmic ensembles—with a variety of electronic "urban" sounds.

ELECTRONICS: PRESERVING AND SPREADING THE TRADITIONS

The recording industry, like that of the West, is now a century old in India. Classical music, because of its extended sense of time, was a latecomer to the scene, and was not seriously thought of as recordable until the advent of the long-playing record in the 1950s. Light music, *ghazals*, *bhajans*, and songs (especially film songs), have also received the greatest attention by the electronic media.

CD track 42 is an excerpt from a recording (*Mirāsim*) by the very popular singer Jagjit Singh that shows the eclectic musical nature of a *ghazal* produced in a modern recording studio. A flute and chordal guitar introduction includes very delicate interjections on a *sitār*. Jagjit-ji, the vocalist, enters, with the first couplet: "Why are there tears in my eyes? I cannot forget the smoke . . . I woke in a cloud, but there was no rain." The *tablā* player subtly makes his entrance along with an understated cymbal. In the break, there is a quick violin interlude (but why does he not sound Western?), followed by an answer on the *sitār*. These instrumental elements are carefully crafted to give pleasing variety and flavor to the texture.

Another approach to the integration of Indian and Western sounds can be heard in the innovative duets of *sitarist* Krishna Bhatt, with the traditional American singer and guitarist Jody Stecher. On CD track 43 they play an old-time fiddle tune, *Yellow Gal*. You also can hear a five-string banjo (Fred Sokolov) and the string bass (Nancy Schenk), and Jody-ji plays a bit of mandolin on the recording as well. While the overall color of the sound is bluegrass, the *sitār* lead is unique. The traditional tune itself is somewhat rhythmically eccentric, having a seven-bar rhythm in its first part. It is uncommon to find such tunes with odd bar counts in most fiddle music intended for dance (but otherwise not unheard-of); certainly it presents no impediment to a musician such as Krishna Bhatt, who hails from the land of rhythmic variety. The structure of the repetitions is AABBA, and this whole tune-pattern takes a mere twenty-two seconds to occur. The artists play the tune three times with minor rhythmic ornaments, and at the 1:07 point, the *sitār* takes a solo variation that slows down the harmonic rhythm, while the other instruments continue strumming in the background. This solo breaks the predictable harmonic pattern of the tune, putting the accompanists on the spot: it was recorded live, and they have to listen and adjust instantly to the "chord changes" implied by the *sitār* solo. This aspect of the music—the tendency to play across regular harmonic rhythms—is one of the main reasons one does not hear more east-west blends. Krishna-ji brings the short solo to an exciting conclusion, melding it perfectly with the reintroduction of the final statement of the tune, played in the heterogeneous style of the beginning, at 1:30.

SOME VIEWS FROM AN OLD MASTER

It is August of 2000. I am at the home of my *guru*-ji, the renowned sarodist Ali Akbar Khansahib, at his home near his College of Music in San Rafael, California, where he has taught for more than thirty years. He lives in a small house in these suburbs of San Francisco, north of the famous Golden Gate Bridge, with his wife and three children. Khansahib often receives visitors in the evening at his home—if there is music to be taught, then one comes early. If not, then one arrives after 8 P.M. His room is on the newly added second floor, above the clamor of his three kids with their neighborhood friends, whose vigorous American lifestyle contrasts with the sanctorum of the master's second floor. There is a couch and a chair in the spacious room, but the chief sitting area is the thick green carpet upon which most of his guests seat themselves on the floor, "Indian style." On one wall is a large curtained bookcase which functions almost like an altar, where Khansahib keeps icons of many religions. There are also many photos and mementos of his more personal spiritual history and quest, but this bookcase will be closed when an informal, conversational, or party atmosphere takes over the room. Khansahib has received many distinguished friends, dignitaries, students, and admirers in this room, and he receives guests with a cordiality that places everyone at ease.

Well, almost at ease. I, for one, am never totally at ease with a man whose musical genius has awed and humbled me on hundreds of occasions. Now in his eighties, he can still produce music of spellbinding invention, lilting charm, fierce power, and profound sadness . . . all in one sitting. And he has taught his tradition freely to everyone who sits in front of him, without regard to their pedigree or musical background—the entire gamut of the repertoire of Hindustani music, from vocal music to instrumental, and from light-classical tunes to the most intricate and mathematical depths of the tradition. In the face of this understanding of this man's stature and gift to mankind, one cannot be casual.

With all that in mind, I volunteer my diffidence at having returned to California to play a program at his College—to play on the very platform from which he has taught thousands of classes.

He laughs. "That is a good sign. A musician has to begin from a feeling of humility, or he will not find that mood." He pauses. We five or six visitors become silent, for this is an area of mutual interest to all of his students. "My father taught that music is like a prayer, you see. When you pray you cannot think, 'Oh, I am great,' 'I am doing all this and all that,' 'My *tān*s are fastest,' and all that macho stuff. You won't get God's grace with that attitude . . . and your music will suffer."

A young student speaks up: "But Khansahib, so many musicians are playing that way. And what else can we do? We have to show the power and speed or else people will be bored."

"No . . . if you play in rhythm and in tune, God will help you. That is my point. If you start by thinking the other way, your music will be hopeless. *That* is boring music. Box-office type music. Many people are doing that, but I don't think that way."

"When I was a boy, in those days people thought of the [classical] music as either *dhrupad style* or *khyāl* style. In *khyāl* style, they did not pay so strict attention to matters of purity in the *rāg*s, and *dhrupad* people, they always were very careful about those things."

"Ding-dong-ding-dong," a clock insolently chimes the half-hour, but Khansahib thoughtfully continues, "My feeling is, that the music is gradually going down and down . . . but it won't die . . . and one day it will come up again, just like it has happened before in history. Sometimes it became less, and people became aware of these things. But then somebody has to show them—what is going wrong—but nowadays the young generation has no idea about this, and the old maestros are not alive."

"When I was growing up, the musicians came to the programs and sat in the front row. When an artist started some monkey business with the *rāga*, they [the older musicians] would shout, right in the performance. Nowadays, there is nobody left like that."

"But today the musicians have to tour all the time, and think about money matters, and entertainment. They don't really have the time to teach in the old way."

We students shuffled nervously and looked at each other in the sighing acknowledgement of the possibility that the great tradition was in an ebbing stage. After a silence, someone piped up, "But Khansahib, a lot of good things are happening, too. I heard you, like, in New York on a recording. I didn't know, like, *anything*, but I was able to get on a plane and come to study with you. *That* couldn't have happened in the old days!"

"Yes, these kinds of things—television, recording, concerts—they are all improving a lot. The publicity matters are better, but at the same time the publicity can spoil the whole thing, and create the wrong idea in everybody's mind. In the old days these things were weak, but the music was more pure. Nowadays, you pick up any magazine, and there are teachers all over. And people are running to learn. But what they are learning is tending to the mixed kind. Not pure. That is my point."

"But so many things are easier today for you-all. Today you have nice microphones, nice concert halls, nice places to learn, airplanes, recordings . . . today you can hear so many artists, like Vilayat Khan, Amir Khan, Ravi Shankar, Bhimsen Joshi, Mallik Arjun Misra . . . but I think these are the last of that standard. How many people of the young generation have put in the time to practice and learn even thirty-five percent of what those older artists did? And many times they are copying the music—using some of this, some from that artist—and mixing it all up, so I say again, you can't keep the purity like that . . ."

For me, it is a sobering contemplation to look one's own future in the eye and think that it all might not ever be what it was. Wordsworth's *Ode* goes through my mind:

Waters on a starry night
Are beautiful and fair
The sunshine is a glorious birth
But yet I know, where'er I go
That there hath passed away a glory from the earth.

"Hmm. Someone has been down this road before," I think. And I muse about the life's work of this great artist sitting before me. Of anyone I know, he certainly dedicated his life and time to passing on the tradition in the purest way he knew. I wonder if anyone in antiquity could have done a better job. Considering the circumstances of trans-generational, multi-artistic, cross-cultural contortion which attended Khansahib's storybook journey—growing up in a feudal court in a traditional culture, suddenly being called upon to address the modern artistic world, and landing amidst the headlong rush of the quilted society we collectively address as twenty-first century America—all of this would be hard work for anyone, and I bring it to his attention now.

"Khansahib, do you look back at your long years of teaching with a sense of satisfaction?"

"Well, I have been teaching for almost sixty years. It makes me sad that some of my finest students, like Brij Bushan Kabra (guitar) and Nikhil Banerjee (*sitār*), are no longer alive. But this group in America and Europe, if they can make the sacrifice in their life to teach and keep the music pure, it will bring another kind of pleasure to the soul . . . but they cannot expect gain. They must know that they are working for a good cause in their life, and that will be good for the future of every generation. And if you get the right kind of students, that is another kind of pleasure, because you also learn at the same time."

"Because this music is not just to entertain, it is really a pathway to God. And once you really get the right sound in your soul and mind, it is such a peaceful and pleasant feeling. That peace you cannot get anywhere."

Glossary

A SIMPLE GUIDE TO PRONUNCIATION OF HINDI

In Hindi, the short a sounds (without the macron-line above the letter) are pronounced with a short "uh" sound, as in the English word "but." Hence the instrument, *tablā*, is pronounced "tub-lāh." A long ā sound (with the line above the a) is pronounced broadly, as in the English word "father." The i has also a long and short form: the i that ends most words is often long. Many consonants have an aspirated form, with and without an h. In a general sense, one can pronounce aspirated consonants with a slightly breathy exhalation afterwards. An aspirated t, for instance, sounds like the th in "Thomas." An unaspirated t sounds like the t in "stop." Specific words below may have a phonetic pronunciation given, if deemed necessary.

Ākār: Singing with an open syllable, "ah".

Ālāp-jor: First movement of a *rāg* performance, characterized by a slow abstract beginning which gathers momentum (*jor*) through use of an accelerating tempo.

Anibaddh-nibaddh: Unbound-bound; referring to both musical sections such as *ālāp* and *gat*, and phrasing which is metrically loose or specific (*nibaddh*).

Antarā: The second part of a composition using the higher register (high **sa** and above).

Asthāī: The "at home" part of a composition, sung or played in the home registers of the *rāg*.

Baḍhāt: "Growth," or the typical unfolding of a composition; likened to the growth of a plant from seed to full flowering (pronounced: "bur-hot").

Baijī: A member of the courtesan class in North India, whose skills often include music, dance, poetry, and social refinement.

Bāj: "Style," or the way in which a rag is rendered.

Bandish: A fixed composition in a *rāg*.

Baṛā: "Great," referring to the slow composition and its exposition of *rāg* in the *khyāl* style (this word is pronounced with the r almost like a d).

Bānsurī: The keyless bamboo flute of North India.

Bhai: "Brother," a common way of address friends in the musical family; also common as a suffix to names.

Bhajan: A devotional hymn; usually in light-classical style.

Bhakti: "Devotion;" it is a major attitude in the discipline of classical music, and also the name of the period between 1450–1650 CE, which has rough parallels to the ideals behind the Protestant Reformation in Europe.

Bhangrā: A folk dance from the Punjab that has gained new life in clubs and performance groups especially in England and the US.

Bharāt Natyam: The name given to a classical dance style that was originally cultivated in the courts and temples of South India, especially in Tamil Nadu.

Bhāva: "Expression"; the chore of the performer is to bring out the bhāva of a given *rāg* in performance.

Bolbānt: Division of the words; in dhrupad style, the section at the end of a *rāga* performance in which the performer creates new melodic and rhythmic patterns using the song text.

Boltān: In khyāl style, the use of the words to create improvised melodic patterns; in instrumental music, the use of rhythmic stroke patterns *(bols)* to create variations.

Carnatic: The great tradition of *rāga* and *tāla* in South India.

Chanchal: "Restless"; A general descriptive term for the mood of most lighter classical music.

Chhand: "Rhythm" in the general sense; in a more specific use, it can refer to multimeter or the grouping of a rhythmic pulse.

Chhotā: "Small"; in khyāl style, the faster composition which usually follows a slow *(bāṛa)* exposition in a *rāg*.

Desī: "Country"; refers to the folk element in the sources of *rāgas*.

Devadāsī: A caste of temple musicians and dancers who nurtured the arts as devotees of Hindu temples.

Dhol: A double-ended, barrel-shaped drum whose sound is often heard in folk and light-classical music.

Dhrupad: A style of music developed in the middle ages in North India consisting of two basic movements: *ālāp-jor* and the *dhrupad*, or fixed song.

Gamak: A style of ornamentation in which a pitch is rapidly intoned or repeated with a quick neighbor note approaches from above or below. Often used to describe ornaments in a more general sense (pronounced: "gummuck").

Gambhīr: A general term to describe a raga whose nature is serious, solemn, or deep.

Gat: A fixed composition for instruments, drumming, or dance, in which contrasting rhythmic bols play a structural function. The term is more generally used to describe the entire part of an instrumental performance that is accompanied by *tablā*.

Gintī: Counting; specifically a rhythmic composition that is articulated by the recitation of numbers in sequential patterns.

Gharāna: A musical style that is handed down through the teaching of a specific lineage of *gurus*. In former times it carried implications of the blood lineage and intermarriage of a musical family.

Ghazal: A poetic format, especially in Urdu, using couplets to express feelings of love devotion. The popular film-song tradition often borrows from this type of lyric.

Great Tradition: The classical music of *rāga* and *tāla* that carries across regional boundaries.

Guru: "Teacher"; often used in a more spiritual sense of a preceptor who leads a student from darkness to light.

Guru-shisyā parampara: The tradition of the teacher and student that connects the training to historical precedents of a particular style.

Hindustāni: The general name for the classical tradition of North India.

Jātī: "Type"; melodic *jātīs* classify scales into pentatonic, hexatonic, and heptatonic structures; and rhythmic *jātīs* classify rhythms according to their 2-3-4-5, etc., pulse structures.

Javarī: The buzzing sound of a metal string against a flat bridge that characterizes the timbre of many Indian stringed instruments.

Jhālā: "Sparkling"; the rapid section, which concludes an instrumental performance that uses repeated striking of the drone strings.

Jī: A suffix added to names denoting respect and affection.

Jor: "Momentum"; the second part of an ālāp in which a rhythmic pulse is introduced, but which has no fixed meter.

Khālī: "Empty"; the section of a rhythmic cycle (*tāla*) which is signified by a wave of the hands.

Khāndān: "Family"; the term used to describe the blood-family connections of a musical *gharānā* (q.v.).

Khyāl: "Imagination"; a vocal style of many varieties that arose in the eighteenth century and has become the prevalent way of rendering classical music.

Laya: "Speed"; tempo in its sense of slow-medium-fast, or relative speed wherein one describes the division of the beat or the ratio between a composition and the *tāla* in which it is set.

Little Tradition: A term to describe regional styles in contrast to the Great Tradition of *rāga* and *tāla*; regional styles may be ancient, refined, and contain a large literature, and hence have "classical" parameters.

Mantrā: A spiritual saying or aphorism, usually in Sanskrit, given by a guru to aid in concentration of the mind during meditation.

Mārga: "Road"; the aspect of the classical tradition in which the spiritual path is manifest through the yoga of learning and practice.

Muezzin: In Islam, the crier who calls the faithful to prayer five times a day, often from a minaret.

Mughal: A dynasty of rulers beginning with Babar in 1526 and extending though 1859, including Akbar the Great, Jehangir, and Shah Jahan.

Mukhrā: "Face"; a phrase of a composition in khyāl style that is used as a refrain or point of return to a fixed composition.

Mukti: "Release"; the concept of salvation in the Hindu faith which is the object of spiritual practice.

Nād-brahmā: "The language of God"; the concept that sound (*nād*) itself is a sacred manifestation of the universe.

Nom-tom: The short form of referring to the syllables of a *dhrupad*-style ālāp: *ta na ri re ra na nom-tom*.

Pakhāwaj: The double-ended, inverted hourglass-shaped drum of the dhrupad tradition.

Pandit: In the Hindu tradition, a term of respect for a person of learning or artistic accomplishment, or a teacher. See *ustād*.

Playback singer: A singer whose music is used in films, while the music is lip-synced by the actors or actresses.

Prakrit: "Nature"; a *rāg's prakrit* is said to lie on a continuum between solemn (*gambhīr*) and restless (*chanchal*).

Qawwālī: A genre of sacred music in Islamic countries of West and South Asia, characterized by the heightened emotional delivery of male singers who often sing in call-and-response formats.

Rāga: *Rāgas* (Hindi: *rāg*) are the melodic formats of classical music in India. Ranging from simple scales to actual compositions, most *rāgs* lie in between these poles. Most suggest melodic ideas loosely interwoven with upward and downward scale motions.

Rāgamāla: In performance, a garland, or medley, of *rāgas*. Historically, *rāgamālas* were a series of miniature paintings romantically depicting the flavor and poetic implications of the *rāgas*.

Rāginī: A female *rāga* from the older classification methods that stated that a certain number of parent *rāgas* would have a given number of wives (*rāginis*), and from them came offspring (*putrās*), which aligned the *rāga* literature into families.

Rasa: "Juice"; used in music to describe the basic moods. They were classified into nine basic types (*navarasa*) in the ancient literature on the dramatic and musical arts.

Riāz: "Practice," especially of arts of musical or dance.

Rīti: The name of the mannerist school of poetry of the seventeenth and eighteenth century that bequeathed a genre of love poetry and imagery to classical song lyrics.

Sādhanā: Spiritual practice—refers especially to the devotional aspect in practicing of the arts of music and dance.

Sanskrit: "Cultured" or "refined"; especially the Sanskrit language, originating in Vedic times, and later developing into a vast classical language of ancient India.

Santūr: A hammered dulcimer of the Middle East that was carried along the Silk Road into northern India.

Sarangī: A bowed lute of thirty-five strings, which was often used to accompany voice and dance, but has had a long solo tradition as well.

Sārgām: The names of the pitches, or a composition or section in which the names of the notes are used. Comparable to solfeggio in the west.

Sarod: One of the primary lutes in Hindustani music. Derived from several types of *rababs,* the *sarod* has a goatskin table and a smooth steel fingerboard upon which the player slides the fingernails of his left hand (pronounced: suh-road").

Sahib: An Islamic term for master also used as a suffix.

Sam: The first beat of a *tāl.*

Shāhnāi: A conical and keyless double-reed instrument of North India originally associated with weddings and festivals, but is now heard on stage in classical performance.

Sitār: The long-necked lute of North India brought to international prominence through the playing of Ravi Shankar, Vilayat Khan, and Nikhil Banerjee.

Svār: Note or pitch. Also, *sūr.*

Tablā: The pair of hand drums, baya and tablā, which have become the most popular drums of the classical tradition.

Taiyārī: "Readiness"; an artist's responsibility is to bring his technique and learning to a plateau of readiness.

Tāla: The system of rhythm in Indian classical music, specifically the rhythmic cycle.

Tān: A melodic pattern used to expand the *rāga* in performance after the fixed composition; often used in the sense of a fast melodic run.

Tānpurā: The stringed drone, the long-necked lute heard in the background of a classical performance; also spelled *tamboura*.

Tarānā: A rhythmic vocal composition in which the abstract syllables, some derived from drumming and dance, are set to a particular *rāga* and *tāla*.

Thekā: The pattern in drum strokes, which identifies, like a signature, a given *tāla*.

Thumrī: A vocal genre developed in the nineteenth century, using light-classical *rāgas*; the characteristically quick filigree ornaments of *thumī* are often heard in shorter compositions played toward the end of a classical performance.

Tihāī: "One-third"; a rhythmic or melodic pattern repeated three times, often returning to the downbeat of the rhythmic cycle.

Tintāl: The most common of the *tāls*; a 16-beat rhythm cycle that is divided into four groups of four beats each.

Ustād: In the Islamic tradition, a title for a respected or learned person or teacher.

Vādī-samvādī: The most important note of a *rāga* (besides the tonic, **sa**) is the *vādī*; it has widely varying structural implications with *the samvādī*, a pitch a fourth or fifth away from the *vādī*.

Veda: "Divine knowledge"; the four Vedas, *Rig-, Sāma-, Yājur-,* and *Atharva-vedas*, are the scriptures of the Aryan peoples and form the basis of later Hinduism.

Vikriti: "Crooked"; the way of permutating the order of syllables in Vedic recitation.

Vīna: In classical literature, any stringed instrument; in more modern times, a long-necked lute which is an ancestor of the sitār. Also *bīn*.

Vistār: "Expansion"; in khyāl style, a way of developing the *rāga* with longer notes and phrases, as opposed to tans, which tend to be in a faster tempo.

Resources

Many of the recording samples on the accompanying CD reveal the difficulty in taking excerpts from the classical music—it does not break down into easily separated divisions, and doing so distorts the overall impression of the music. A truer feeling for the styles and *rāgas* that are on this CD can only be had by listening to the entire original recordings. The producers and artists on this collection have been very generous in allowing use of their music, and one hopes that the small glimpses given here will whet the appetite to purchase the entire CD. Often these can be easily ordered through the websites given below. Alam-Medina, Moment, Raga, and Navras are specific Western companies with extensive classical selections.

Alam-Medina Music Productions (http://www.ammp.com/catalog.html, distributed by Revolver USA (415) 241-2437)
AMMP CD 9002 *Rag Chandranandan*, Ali Akbar Khan, *sarod*, with Mahapurush Misra, *tablā* (CD tracks 32–36).
MJK CDF 9601 *Tarānā in Rāg Adāna*, from the CD *Legacy*, sung by Asha Bhosle, with Swapan Chaudhuri, *tablā* (CD track 12).
MJK CDF 9601 *Khyal in Rāg Gaur Sarang*, from the CD *Legacy*, sung by Asha Bhosle, with Ali Akbar Khan, *sarod*; Ramesh Misra, *sarangī*; and Swapan Chaudhuri, *tablā* (CD track 24).

Barenreiter Music Corporation
BM 30 L 2006 (out of print LP recording) *Hymn to Kubera, Hymn to the Moon,* and *Black Yajur Veda,* from *Music of the Orient 6, India 1* (CD tracks 4, 5, 6).

Gramophone Company of India (HMV)
CDF 1.32030 *Mera Saaya Sath Hoga* from *Great Artiste Great Hits,* Lata Mangeshkar, vocal; Madan Mohan, music producer (CD track 1).

Moment Records (http://www.momentrecords.com/)
MRCD 1001 *Ustad Alla Rakha and Zakir Hussain, tablā* duet, with Ramesh Misra, *sarangī,* recorded in concert in Calcutta, January, 1991 (CD track 23).
MRCD 1017 *Rāg Bageshri,* Rashid Khan, vocal; Ananda Gopal Bandopadhyaya, *tablā;* Jyoti Goho, harmonium (CD tracks 25–29).
MRCD 1010 *Rāg Rageshri,* Shivkumar Sharma, *santūr;* Zakir Hussain, *tablā* (CD track 38).
MRCD 1006 *Rajasthani Folksong,* Sultan Khan, *sarangī;* Zakir Hussain, *tablā* (CD track 39).
Unreleased, *Rāg Sanjshravani,* Vilayat Khan, *sitār,* with Zakir Hussain, *tablā* (CD track 30).

Navras Records (http://www.navrasrecords.com/)
NRCD 0007 *Rāg Jāyatshrshrī* Hariprasad Chaurasia, *bansurī;* Fazal Qureshi, *tablā* (CD track 40).

Raga Records (http://www.raga.com/)
Raga 220 *Rāg Todi,* Mohinuddin and Aminuddin Dagar, *dhrupad* vocal; Purushottam Das, *pakhāwaj,* recorded live in Calcutta, 1957 (CD tracks 7–11).
Raga 212 AB *Rāg Sindhūr Khammaj,* Nikhil Banerjee, *sitār,* with Zamir Ahmed Khan, *tablā,* recorded live in Amsterdam, 1972 (CD track 37).

Rooster Records
Rooster LP 115 *Yellow Gal* from Rasa, Krishna Bhatt and Jody Stecher, with Fred Sokolov and Nancy Schenk. Currently out-of-print, plans are underway to reprint this LP recording on CD. (CD track 43).

Rounder Records Corp. (http://www.rounder.com/)
CD 1083 *Fana kaisi bana kaisi* from *Vintage Music from India,* Janki Bai, vocal, recorded in 1908 (CD track 31).

Sony Music Entertainment (India) (http://www.sonymusic.co.in/)
494717 2 *Ankhon mein jal rahe hai kyon* from *Mirasim,* Jagjit Singh, vocal (CD track 42).

Toronto Tabla Ensemble (http://www.tablaensemble.com/)
TTE CD001 *Tongue Twister,* Toronto Tabla Ensemble, Ritesh Das, director (CD track 14).
TTE CD002 *Sample This,* Toronto Tabla Ensemble, *Sample This,* Ritesh Das, director (CD track 41).

Universal Music India (formerly Polygram India) (http://www.universal-music.com/)
CDNF 332 *Maine lino Govind* from *Bhajan Ganga,* Anup Jalota, vocal (CD track 13).

Written Sources

Coomaraswamy, Ananda. 1957. *The Dance of Shiva: Fourteen Indian Essays.* New York: Noonday Press.
Mehta, Gita. 1993. *A River Sutra.* New York: Random House.
Shankar, Ravi. 1992. *My Music, My Life.* Delhi: Vikas Publishing House.
————. 1997. *Ragamala.* New York: Welcome Rain Publishers.

Locating Sources

There are innumerable websites to check for the distribution of musical instruments, books, and recordings of Indian music. One might begin a search in the United States with the following sites.

Ali Akbar College of Music Store
415 West End Ave.
San Rafael, CA 94901
(800) 748-2252
http://www.aacm.org/shop/

Shrimati's Compact Disks
2011 University Ave.
Berkeley, CA 94704
http://www.shrimatis.com/updates/cdpdflist.htm

South Asia Books
P.O. Box 502
Columbia, MO 65205
(573) 474-0116
http://www.southasiabooks.com/

Index